METABASE 101

All you need to setup your open source business intelligence system

First Edition

Copyright

About the Author

Tran Duc Loi aka *Leo Tran* is a fan of minimalism and an enthusiast Python programmer since 2014 when he accidentally asked to join a new Python community with some friends.

Beside Python, he also added JavaScript to his stack with React JS for frontend and React Native for mobile development.

By the same Author

- Python For Desktop Applications - How to develop, pack and deliver Python applications with TkInter and Kivy
- METABASE 101 – Everything you need to setup your open source business intelligence system

Table of Contents

Preface

What this book covers

Chapter 1, Installing Metabase shows you how to install a **Metabase** using a **JAR** file, using a **Docker** container, deploying on **Heroku** cloud, changing default backend **H2** database to **Postgres**, migrating from the installed **H2** to a new **Postgres** database, adding **Oracle** & **CSV** drivers. At the end of this chapter, you will have an up & running **Metabase**.

Chapter 2, Adding Data Sources introduces how to add various kinds of data sources to a **Metabase**: CSV files, **MySQL**, **Oracle** database …

Chapter 3, Basic Configurations walks through additional configurations needed for the **Metabase**. Authentication using **LDAP**, **Google Authentication**, email, **Slack**, and some fine-tuning configurations to help your **Metabase** more secured.

Chapter 4, Users, Groups, and Permissions addresses how to adapt a **Metabase** to your organization's hierarchy. You will be guided to create users, groups, and permissions based on the pre-defined hierarchy. Compounding with *Analytics, Collections, and Reports* in *Chapter 5*, you will know how the whole **Metabase** reporting system works.

Chapter 6, Advanced Metabase helps you with some more difficult techniques like XRAY, native queries, regional maps, pin maps, data models, data hiding, troubleshooting, and multi-instance synchronization.

This book expresses my experience working with **Metabase** to build complete BI systems for small to medium companies. All the illustrations in the book have been conducted by myself.

What will you need for this book

In this book, we'll use:

- **Metabase** 0.37.6 (*not the latest version*)
- **Java JDK 8** (*to run Metabase from a JAR file locally*)
- **Docker Desktop** with **Docker Engine** v20.10.2 (*to install Metabase using Docker - optional*)
- A free account at **https://www.heroku.com** (*to deploy Metabase on Heroku cloud - optional*)
- **ojdbc8.jar** (*to connect to Oracle database - optional*)
- **csv.metabase-driver.jar** version 1.0.2 (*to use CSV files as your data source - optional*)
- **Microsoft Visual Code 1.49.0** as main editor (*optional*)

All the packages/tools are free at the time of writing. You don't have to search and download those tools yourself right now, we will have one chapter to guide you on how to set them up with very detailed information.

Who this book is for

This book is for any person that may start from zero.

You don't need to be a programmer, a data analyst, or a SQL expert to use this book. Although it will be easier to read this book if you have some skills related to databases, I believe that you can achieve more if you do practice all guides in the book.

I, myself, have done all the demos before writing any guide in this book to make sure all of them work seamlessly.

At any level, I recommend you try to explore all reference links at the end of each chapter.

How to use this book

This is a *practical* book. That means you will need to get your hands dirty.

You need to:

1. Install the required tools.
2. Clone the the book's Github repository. During the setup of **Metabase**, we will use some resources that I've dedicatedly created for this book.
3. Practice the guides in all chapters.
4. Tweak the settings to see all the features of **Metabase**.
5. Read the notes to understand deeply, follow the links for more detail.
6. Change the settings to adapt your purposes.
7. Join the official Telegram chat group of the book for more support.

This book is a step-by-step guide from the beginning to a complete usable, extensible, production-ready reporting system, so I recommend you read and practice chapter-by-chapter.

Conventions

This book has some conventions that you should be familiar with to get more from this book.

 One of my favourite wheel libraries is:
https://www.lfd.uci.edu/~gohlke/pythonlibs/

This is an information box, tips, and tricks. I usually explain things and answer some common questions here. It is an interesting box.

```
12    # --------------------------------------
13
14    import datetime, os, sys, platform
15
16    def hello():
17        print("Hello, this is Python version", 
```

This is the source code of the examples. We need the line number as we will use line numbers as an anchor to explain the code.

```
D:\setup>java -jar metabase.0.37.6.jar
```

This is a command that runs in PowerShell or Command-line (in Windows) or Terminal (Linux).

your data better from a unified web interface.

well-known **Power BI**, **Tableau** and **Oracle BI**,

File names, commands, folder names, software names, technologies usually use bold format with different font family than normal text just to emphasize them.

Reader feedback

All feedback about the content of the book should be sent to the Telegram group at https://t.me/metabase101 or emailed directly the author at loitranduc@gmail.com. Let us know what you think about this book – what you liked or may have disliked.

To give any feedback about the source code, please:

- To find support interactively, chat with us at https://t.me/metabase101 (the official book's Telegram group)
- If you don't think you can provide a patch, open a New Issue at: https://github.com/loitd/metabase101/issues
- If you think you can make some patch/fix the issue, fork the repository and make a Pull Request at: https://github.com/loitd/metabase101/pulls.
- Please don't email me problems with source code. It should be done using the Github tool.

 For more information about Github flow, please refer to: https://docs.github.com/en/free-pro-team@latest/github/collaborating-with-issues-and-pull-requests

Reader feedback is important for us to develop titles that you really get the most out of.

Downloading example code

All the resources in the book can be found at https://github.com/loitd/metabase101. You should use **git clone https://github.com/loitd/metabase101** command or download directly from the Github repository.

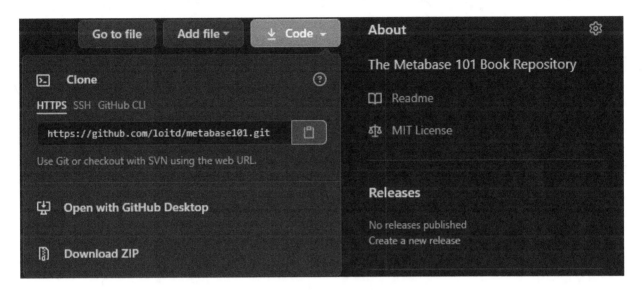

Figure 1. Downloading source from Github repository

This page intentionally left blank

Chapter 1: Installing Metabase

This chapter shows you how to install a **Metabase** using a **JAR** file, using a **Docker** container, deploying on **Heroku** cloud, changing default backend **H2** database to **Postgres**, migrating from the installed **H2** to a new **Postgres** database, and adding **Oracle** & **CSV** drivers. At the end of this chapter, you will have an up & running **Metabase.**

1.1. Introduction

Metabase (metabase.com) is an easy-to-install, open-source business intelligence solution that helps you understand your data better from a unified web interface.

In the same field, we have had well-known **Power BI**, **Tableau** and **Oracle BI**, etc.

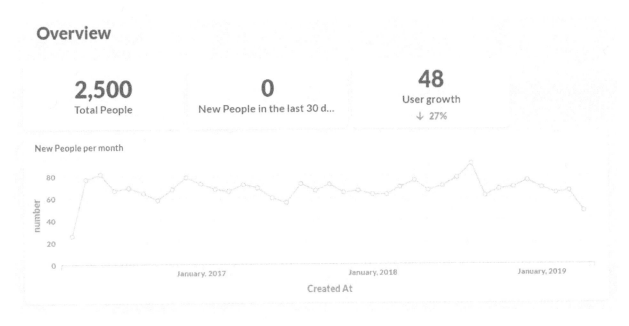

Figure 2. A sample Metabase dashboard

Metabase's backend database

To help you not being confused:

- **Backend databases**: The databases that **Metabase** uses to store installation information, permissions, created user accounts, configurations, will use the **H2** database by default. Without a backend database, you can't start **Metabase** up.
- **Data sources**: In this book, they aim to be the databases, files, data stream... those **Metabase** gets data from to form reports, analysis... You can always start **Metabase** up with or without data sources present. The analysis relies on the data sources that will be affected.

You can start a **Metabase** using a non-default database such as **Postgres**, **MySQL**... and you can also migrate from the current running **H2** database to other databases.

Metabase drivers

`Metabase` has some drivers by default those used to connect to various kinds of data sources:

- `Amazon Redshift`
- `BigQuery`
- `Druid`
- `Google Analytics`
- `H2`
- `MongoDB`
- `MySQL`
- `Postgres SQL`
- `Presto`
- `Snowflake`
- `Spark SQL`
- `SQL Server`
- `SQLite`

You can check the list of the current supported drivers using **`Admin Menu`** > **Databases** > **Add Database**:

Figure 3. Some Metabase drivers

Oracle database & **CSV** files are not supported by default. In this chapter, I will show you how to install **Oracle** & **CSV** drivers to a **Metabase** so we can connect to **Oracle** & **CSV** databases.

Choosing Metabase version

The latest version of **Metabase** at the time of writing is **v0.38.0.1**. Because of some bugs in adding custom maps in this version, in this book, we will use **v0.37.6**. You can check your **Metabase** version in the **About Metabase** dialog.

Figure 4. Checking Metabase version

The bug can be found here:

- https://github.com/metabase/metabase/issues/14635
- https://discourse.metabase.com/t/custom-map-not-working/13303

The error screen will be something like this:

Figure 5. The Metabase custom map bug

Metabase pricing options

Metabase provides two main options:

- **Metabase** cloud with 3 packages:
    - Startup
    - Business
    - Enterprise
- **Metabase** on-premise that you host **Metabase** software yourself with 2 options:
    - Open Source (*what we will use in this book*)
    - Enterprise

The pricing plans at the time of writing:

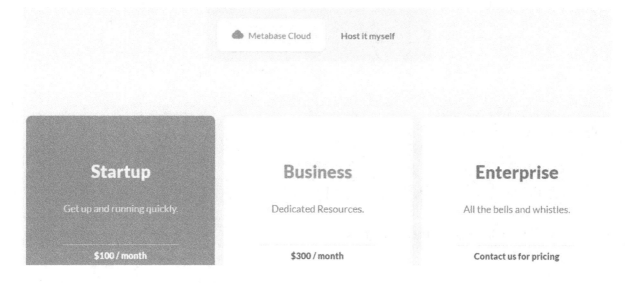

Figure 6. Metabase cloud pricing

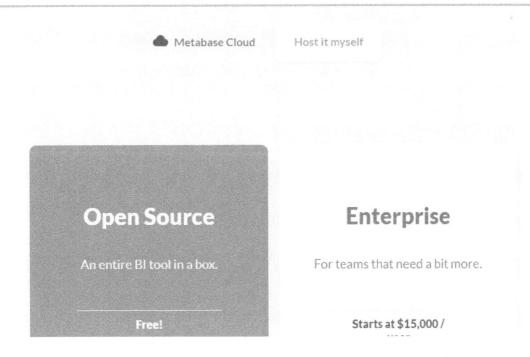

Figure 7. Metabase on-premise pricing

For more detail, you can check on **Metabase**'s homepage: metabase.com.

1.2. Metabase Installation

The **Metabase** open-source on-premise version supports several ways to deploy:

- From a JAR file (within Java environment)
- On macOS as a macOS application
- A Docker container
- AWS Elastic Beanstalk
- Heroku
- Kubernetes

For the complete list of **Metabase** installation methods, you can check at Metabase installation page.

Installing Metabase from a JAR file

Download the JAR file (with a specific version at the download link as we are not using the latest one): https://downloads.metabase.com/v0.37.6/metabase.jar

Download and install **Java JDK 8** at:
https://www.oracle.com/in/java/technologies/javase/javase-jdk8-downloads.html

On the download page, choose which Java for your operating system. In my examples in this book, I am using Windows 10 64 bit.

| Windows x86 | 154.69 MB | ⬇ jdk-8u281-windows-i586.exe |
| Windows x64 | 166.97 MB | ⬇ jdk-8u281-windows-x64.exe |

Figure 8. Choosing Java JDK version

You may need log in Oracle to download. After installing Java, check the installation with this command:

```
D:\setup>java -version
java version "1.8.0_281"
Java(TM) SE Runtime Environment (build 1.8.0_281-b09)
Java HotSpot(TM) 64-Bit Server VM (build 25.281-b09, mixed mode)
```

Then start **Metabase** using the below command:

```
D:\setup>java -jar metabase.0.37.6.jar
```

The output will be something like this:

```
D:\setup>java -jar metabase.0.37.6.jar
2021-03-03 16:42:22,653 INFO metabase.util :: Maximum memory avai.
2021-03-03 16:42:46,779 INFO util.encryption :: Saved credentials
 For more information, see https://metabase.com/docs/latest/opera
2021-03-03 16:43:04,463 INFO metabase.core ::
Metabase v0.37.6 (344e5e0 release-x.37.x)

Copyright - 2021 Metabase, Inc.


... (Omitted output)


2021-03-03 16:43:15,525 INFO metabase.task :: Initializing task SyncDatabases
2021-03-03 16:43:15,880 INFO metabase.task :: Initializing task CheckForNewVersions
2021-03-03 16:43:15,955 INFO metabase.task :: Initializing task SendAnonymousUsageStats
2021-03-03 16:43:16,076 INFO metabase.task :: Initializing task SendAbandomentEmails
2021-03-03 16:43:16,115 INFO metabase.task :: Initializing task SendPulses
2021-03-03 16:43:16,245 INFO metabase.task :: Initializing task SendFollowUpEmails
2021-03-03 16:43:16,510 INFO metabase.task :: Initializing task TaskHistoryCleanup
2021-03-03 16:43:16,614 INFO metabase.core :: Metabase Initialization COMPLETE
2021-03-03 16:43:21,825 INFO i18n.impl :: Reading available locales from locales.clj...
```

By default, **Metabase** will bind to port **3000**, if you want to change the binding port, set the **MB_JETTY_PORT** environment variable to a new destination port before starting **Metabase**:

- In Windows: **set MB_JETTY_PORT=3001**
- On Linux: **export MB_JETTY_PORT=3001**

```
D:\setup>set MB_JETTY_PORT=3001

D:\setup>java -jar metabase.0.37.6.jar
2021-03-02 13:59:29,424 INFO metabase.util :: Maximum memory available to JVM: 779.0 MB
2021-03-02 13:59:43,760 INFO util.encryption :: Saved credentials encryption is DISABLE
 For more information, see https://metabase.com/docs/latest/operations-guide/encrypting
2021-03-02 14:00:10,123 INFO metabase.core ::
Metabase v0.37.6 (344e5e0 release-x.37.x)

Copyright - 2021 Metabase, Inc.
```

In this setup, I will use default port **3000**. Now open your browser and navigate
http://localhost:3000/

Welcome to Metabase

Looks like everything is working. Now let's get to know you, connect to your data, and start finding you some answers!

Let's get started

Figure 9. The Metabase welcome screen

Press the **Let's get started** button

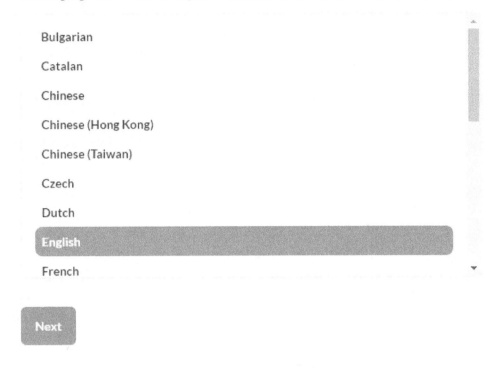

Figure 10. Choosing your preferred language

Choose your preferred language and press the **Next** button

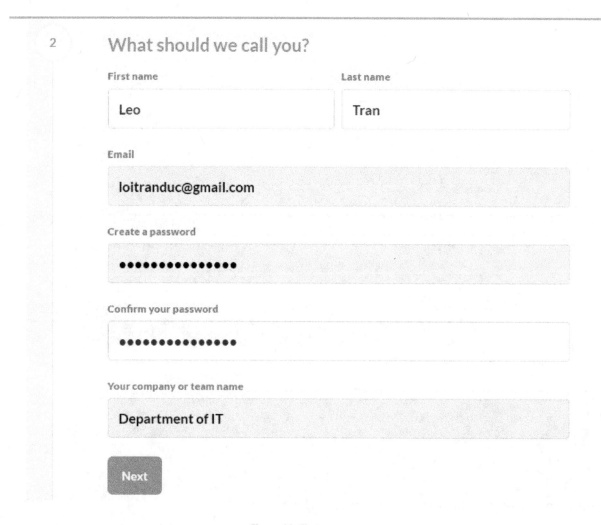

Figure 11. First user setup

Fill in your information then next:

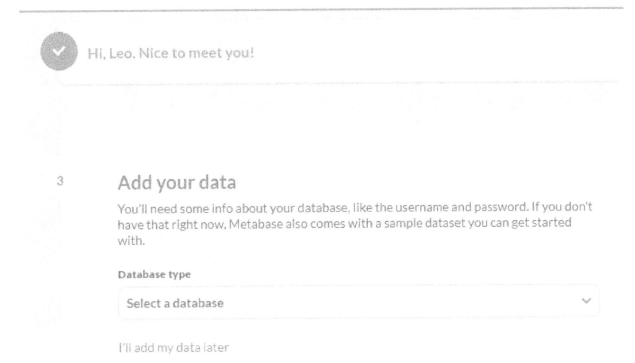

Figure 12. Adding an initial database

Press the **I'll add my data later** link since we can add our data sources later

Figure 13. Usage data preferences

Press **Next** and you're done installing **Metabase**. You will be redirected to the home page.

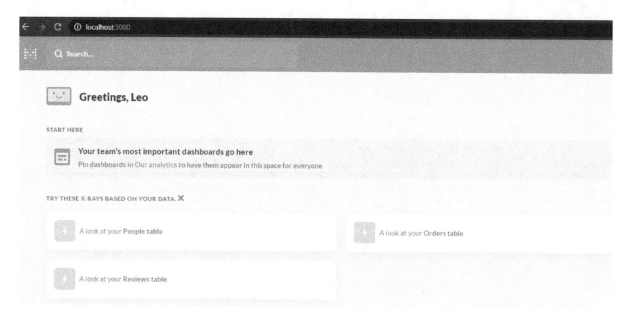

Figure 14. The default dashboard

Within the same folder with the `metabase.jar` file, you now will see some newly added files:

Figure 15. Metabase H2 database

They are the **Metabase's H2** database files created automatically by default during the installation process. You can change to **MySQL** or **Postgres** database later.

 Most of the time, we will not use the **H2** database on a **Metabase** production system.

H2 is a relational database management system written in **Java**. It can be embedded in **Java** applications or run in client-server mode. The software is available as open-source software Mozilla Public License 2.0 or the original Eclipse Public License.

Installing Metabase using Docker

We can easily start **Metabase** using **Docker** with just one command as follow:

```
D:\setup>docker run -d -p 3001:3000 --name metabase metabase/metabase
```

The output will be something like this:

```
D:\setup>docker run -d -p 3001:3000 --name metabase metabase/metabase
Unable to find image 'metabase/metabase:latest' locally
latest: Pulling from metabase/metabase
801bfaa63ef2: Pull complete
9ea1a86b56bd: Pull complete
4a1d10b9682a: Pull complete
4724068bed90: Pull complete
54394035758e: Pull complete
a738051a88c8: Pull complete
Digest: sha256:62a243ceac27fd93b6d8856f81742e3b3623ea5f2f7124517b0824d4722a9511
Status: Downloaded newer image for metabase/metabase:latest
db2e0e66aa7ebc1e59797fd39cac9b14e1dd52c5fda1dc9f796a35ec338480f0
```

In the above command, I start a container from the official **Metabase** docker image and map with port **3001** locally. We now got a familiar setup screen of **Metabase** and you can proceed as we did in the previous section.

Check again in the docker dashboard:

Figure 16. Metabase on docker

To see the console log of **Metabase**, we can use the **docker log -f metabase** command:

```
D:\setup>docker logs -f metabase
Warning: environ value jdk-11.0.10+9 for key :java-version has been overwritten with 11.0.10
WARNING: sun.reflect.Reflection.getCallerClass is not supported. This will impact performance
2021-03-02 07:12:37,674 INFO metabase.util :: Maximum memory available to JVM: 682.0 MB
2021-03-02 07:13:08,280 INFO util.encryption :: Saved credentials encryption is DISABLED for
 For more information, see https://metabase.com/docs/latest/operations-guide/encrypting-datak
2021-03-02 07:13:25,446 INFO metabase.core ::
Metabase v0.38.0.1 (0635914 release-x.38.x)

Copyright © 2021 Metabase, Inc.

Metabase Enterprise Edition extensions are NOT PRESENT.
2021-03-02 07:13:25,462 WARN metabase.core :: WARNING: You have enabled namespace tracing, wh
ormation like db passwords
```

Deploying Metabase on Heroku

To deploy on **Heroku**, you can use one-click deployment link as below:

https://dashboard.heroku.com/new?template=https%3A%2F%2Fgithub.com%2Fmetabase%2F
metabase-deploy

Basically, it's a **Heroku** deployment from a git repository at
https://github.com/metabase/metabase-deploy#master. All you need is a free account of
Heroku. The next screen will be something like this:

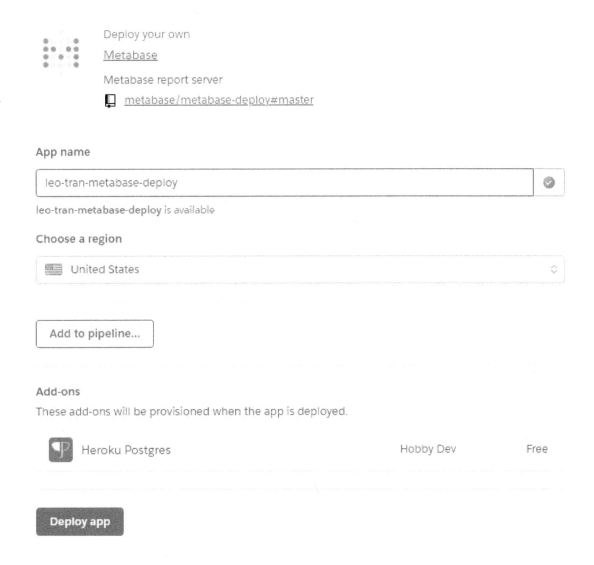

Figure 17. The Heroku one-click deployment (1)

Fill in the name and press the **Deploy app** button. Wait for a while for **Heroku** to deploy:

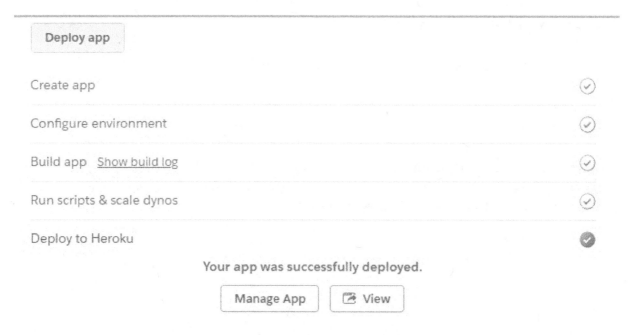

Figure 18. The Heroku one-click deployment (2)

Press the **View** button to access the **Metabase** website, press the **Manage App** button to manage the new **Heroku** app.

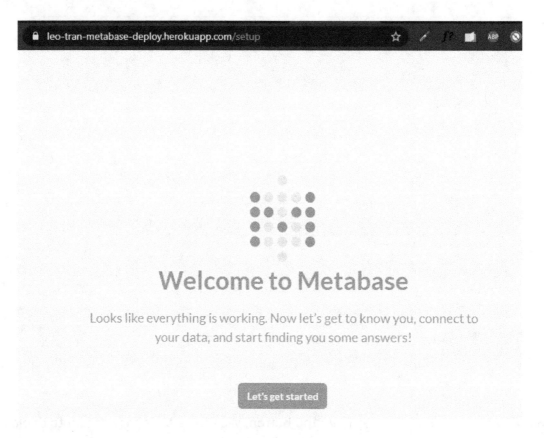

Figure 19. The Metabase setup screen on Heroku

We have our familiar **Metabase** setup page as above.

Check application information at the **Heroku** dashboard:

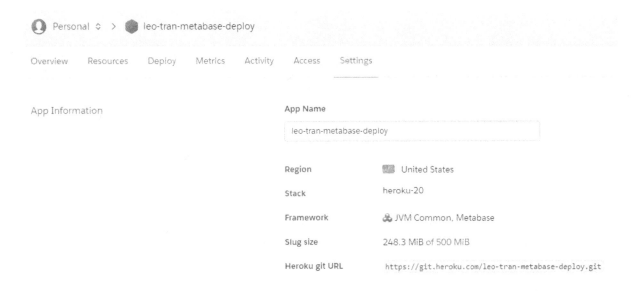

Figure 20. Managing a Metabase application on Heroku

Adding the Oracle driver

By default, **Metabase** does not support connecting to an **Oracle** database. If you want to connect to the Oracle database, you need to install an additional **Oracle** driver. The official document is at: https://www.metabase.com/docs/latest/administration-guide/databases/oracle.html.

Step 1: Download the **ojdbc8.jar** file from Oracle:

Choose any link from these:

- https://www.oracle.com/technetwork/database/application-development/jdbc/downloads/index.html
- Maven Repos:
  https://repo1.maven.org/maven2/com/oracle/database/jdbc/ojdbc8/19.9.0.0/ojdbc8-19.9.0.0.jar

Step 2: Save the **ojdbc8.jar** file into **PLUGINS** folder at the same folder with **metabase.jar** file and restart **Metabase**. If the **PLUGINS** folder doesn't exist, create a new empty one.

Name	Date modified	Type	Size
bigquery.metabase-driver.jar	1/13/2021 10:48 PM	Executable Jar File	623 KB
druid.metabase-driver.jar	1/13/2021 10:48 PM	Executable Jar File	496 KB
google.metabase-driver.jar	1/13/2021 10:48 PM	Executable Jar File	1,037 KB
googleanalytics.metabase-driver.jar	1/13/2021 10:48 PM	Executable Jar File	720 KB
mongo.metabase-driver.jar	1/13/2021 10:48 PM	Executable Jar File	4,531 KB
ojdbc8.jar	3/5/2021 9:30 AM	Executable Jar File	4,306 KB
oracle.metabase-driver.jar	1/13/2021 10:48 PM	Executable Jar File	75 KB
presto.metabase-driver.jar	1/13/2021 10:48 PM	Executable Jar File	163 KB
redshift.metabase-driver.jar	1/13/2021 10:48 PM	Executable Jar File	2,374 KB
snowflake.metabase-driver.jar	1/13/2021 10:48 PM	Executable Jar File	29,503 KB
sparksql.metabase-driver.jar	1/13/2021 10:48 PM	Executable Jar File	61,055 KB
sqlite.metabase-driver.jar	1/13/2021 10:48 PM	Executable Jar File	6,965 KB
sqlserver.metabase-driver.jar	1/13/2021 10:48 PM	Executable Jar File	1,213 KB
vertica.metabase-driver.jar	1/13/2021 10:48 PM	Executable Jar File	55 KB

Figure 21. The OJDBC8 inside Plugins folder

Please note that **Metabase** has **oracle.metabase-driver.jar** by default but you can't use this JAR file as a driver to connect to Oracle.

Now start the **Metabase** and check the console you will see something like this:

```
2021-03-05 09:42:54,114 INFO plugins.dependencies :: Metabase Oracle Driver dependency {:class oracle
isfied? true
2021-03-05 09:42:54,115 DEBUG plugins.lazy-loaded-driver :: Registering lazy loading driver :oracle..
2021-03-05 09:42:54,229 INFO driver.impl :: Registered abstract driver :sql-jdbc (parents: [:sql])
Load driver :sql-jdbc took 119.5 ms
2021-03-05 09:42:54,236 INFO driver.impl :: Registered driver :oracle (parents: [:sql-jdbc])
2021-03-05 09:42:54,243 DEBUG plugins.lazy-loaded-driver :: Registering lazy loading driver :presto..
2021-03-05 09:42:54,245 INFO driver.impl :: Registered driver :presto (parents: [:sql])
2021-03-05 09:42:54,256 DEBUG plugins.lazy-loaded-driver :: Registering lazy loading driver :redshift
2021-03-05 09:42:54,272 INFO driver.impl :: Registered driver :postgres (parents: [:sql-jdbc])
```

Check again on the web UI:

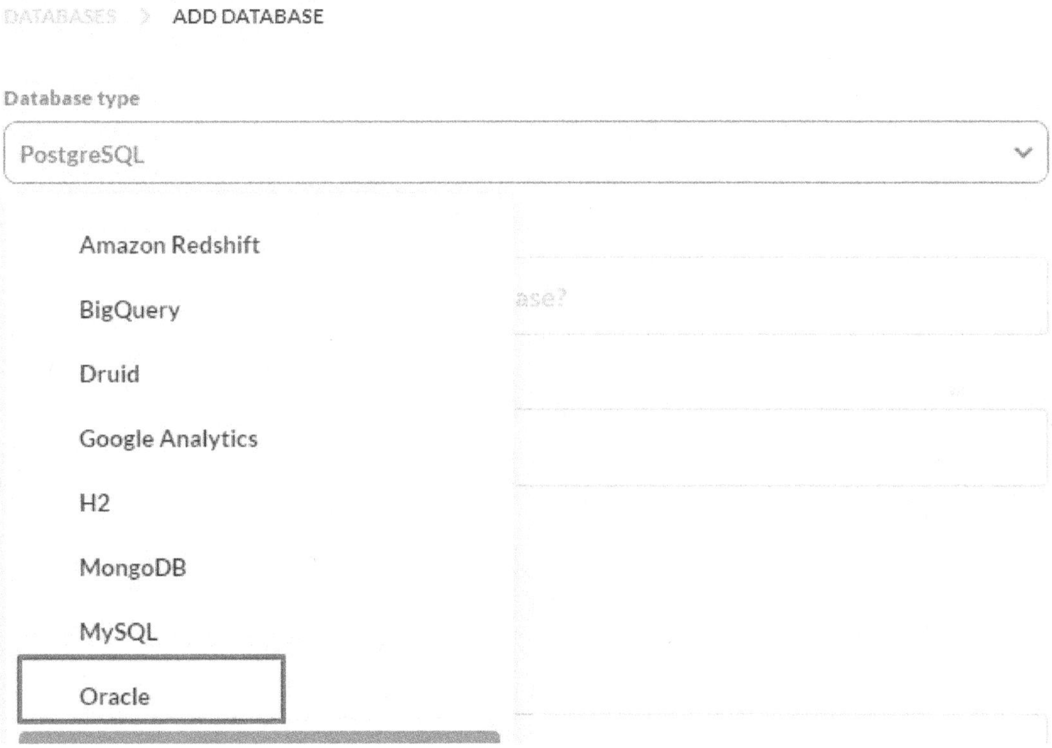

DATABASES > ADD DATABASE

Database type

PostgreSQL ⌄

Amazon Redshift

BigQuery

Druid

Google Analytics

H2

MongoDB

MySQL

Oracle

Figure 22. A Metabase with Oracle driver installed

Adding the CSV driver

In the same process with installing the **Oracle** driver, we will add the CSV driver to our installed **Metabase** with the following simple steps.

Step 1: Download the driver at: https://github.com/Markenson/csv-metabase-driver/releases/download/1.1.0/csv.metabase-driver.jar.

 Please use **exactly CSV Metabase driver version 1.1.0**. I have tried CSV driver version **1.0.2** and it's unable to import CSV files.

Step 2: Save the file into the **PLUGINS** folder. Create the folder if not exist then restart **Metabase**.

Now you will have something like this on the console output:

```
Load driver :sql took 211.4 ms
2021-03-05 09:55:03,191 INFO driver.impl :: Registered abstract driver :sql-jdbc (parents
Load driver :sql-jdbc took 350.2 ms
2021-03-05 09:55:03,201 INFO driver.impl :: Registered driver :csv (parents: [:sql-jdbc])
2021-03-05 09:55:03,213 DEBUG plugins.lazy-loaded-driver :: Registering lazy loading driv
2021-03-05 09:55:03,216 INFO driver.impl :: Registered driver :druid
```

Check the web UI:

Figure 23. Adding the CSV Driver to an existing Metabase

Using Postgres as the backend database

We can set a **Metabase** up using another backend database instead of the default **H2** database. In this setup, I will guide you to install a **Metabase** with **Postgres** as the backend database.

I have had a **Postgres 13.2** database installed with the **metabase** user on the **metabase** database. We will set a new **Metabase** up using this database by setting environment variables.

- On Windows:

    - `SET MB_DB_TYPE=postgres`
    - `SET MB_DB_NAME=metabase`
    - `SET MB_DB_PORT=5432`
    - `SET MB_DB_USER=metabase`
    - `SET MB_DB_PASS=123456`
    - `SET MB_DB_HOST=localhost`

- On Linux:

    - `EXPORT MB_DB_TYPE=postgres`
    - `EXPORT MB_DB_NAME=metabase`
    - `EXPORT MB_DB_PORT=5432`
    - `EXPORT MB_DB_USER=metabase`
    - `EXPORT MB_DB_PASS=123456`
    - `EXPORT MB_DB_HOST=localhost`

Now start **Metabase**

```
D:\setup>set MB_DB_TYPE=postgres

D:\setup>set MB_DB_NAME=metabase

D:\setup>set MB_DB_PORT=5432

D:\setup>set MB_DB_USER=metabase

D:\setup>set MB_DB_PASS=123456

D:\setup>set MB_DB_HOST=localhost

D:\setup>java -jar metabase.0.37.6.jar
2021-03-02 15:19:43,764 INFO metabase.util :: Maximum memory available to JVM: 779.0 MB
2021-03-02 15:19:58,627 INFO util.encryption :: Saved credentials encryption is DISABLEI
 For more information, see https://metabase.com/docs/latest/operations-guide/encrypting-
2021-03-02 15:20:11,744 INFO metabase.core ::
Metabase v0.37.6 (344e5e0 release-x.37.x)

Copyright - 2021 Metabase, Inc.

Metabase Enterprise Edition extensions are NOT PRESENT.
```

… Omitted output

```
2021-03-02 15:20:13,922 INFO metabase.db :: Verifying postgres Database Connection ...
2021-03-02 15:20:13,932 INFO driver.impl :: Initializing driver :sql...
2021-03-02 15:20:13,933 INFO driver.impl :: Initializing driver :sql-jdbc...
2021-03-02 15:20:13,934 INFO driver.impl :: Initializing driver :postgres...
2021-03-02 15:20:14,429 INFO metabase.db :: Successfully verified PostgreSQL 13.2 applic
2021-03-02 15:20:14,434 INFO metabase.db :: Running Database Migrations...
2021-03-02 15:20:14,517 INFO metabase.db :: Setting up Liquibase...
2021-03-02 15:20:15,020 INFO metabase.db :: Liquibase is ready.
2021-03-02 15:20:15,021 INFO db.liquibase :: Checking if Database has unrun migrations..
```

… Omitted output

```
2021-03-02 15:20:40,405 INFO sync.util :: FINISHED: step 'classify-tables' for h2 Databa
2021-03-02 15:20:40,431 INFO sync.util :: FINISHED: Analyze data for h2 Database 1 'Samp
2021-03-02 15:20:40,436 INFO sync.util :: STARTING: Cache field values in h2 Database 1
2021-03-02 15:20:40,440 INFO sync.util :: STARTING: step 'update-field-values' for h2 Da
2021-03-02 15:20:41,634 INFO sync.util :: FINISHED: step 'update-field-values' for h2 Da
2021-03-02 15:20:41,641 INFO sync.util :: FINISHED: Cache field values in h2 Database 1
2021-03-02 15:20:41,642 INFO sync.util :: FINISHED: Sync h2 Database 1 'Sample Dataset'
2021-03-02 15:20:41,647 INFO metabase.core :: Metabase Initialization COMPLETE
```

Now you can check our **Postgres** database administration page:

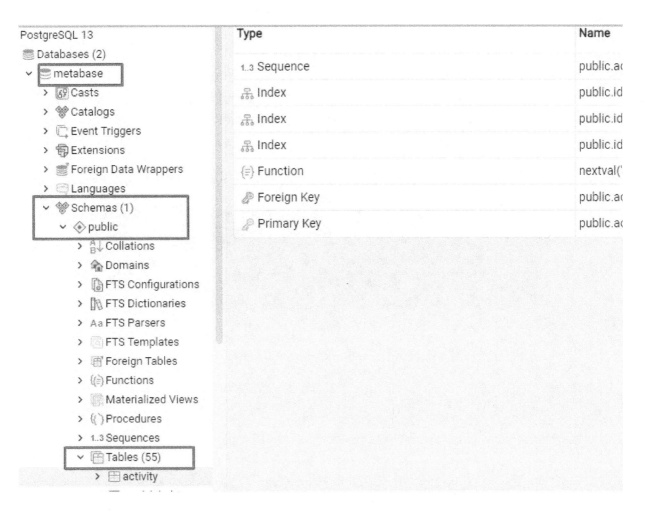

Figure 24. A Metabase using a backend Postgres database

Migrating from H2 to Postgres

As mentioned above, by default, **Metabase** will use an **H2** database. You can also set **Metabase** up with **Postgres** for more production-ready as guided in the previous section. In this section, I will show you how to migrate a **Metabase** system from a running **H2** database to a new **Postgress** database.

We have a **Metabase** with **H2** is running on port 3000. I also have added a new normal user:

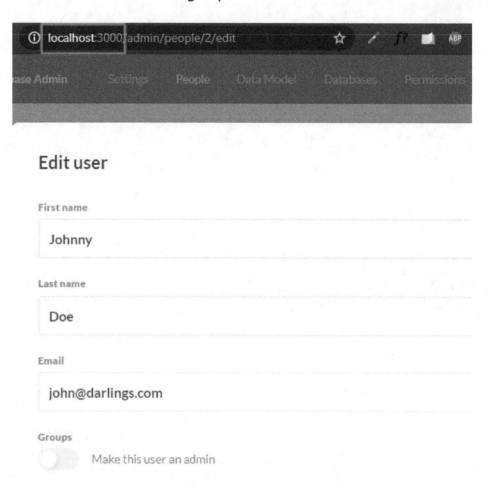

Figure 25. Adding a new user to Metabase

Now we need to stop the current running **Metabase** before doing the migration. Don't forget to stop running **Metabase** or you will get the "`Database may be already in use`" exception.

```
    at org.h2.mvstore.MVStore$Builder.open(MVStore.java:2934)
    at org.h2.mvstore.db.MVTableEngine$Store.open(MVTableEngine.java:155)
    ... 48 more
Command failed with exception: Database may be already in use: null. Possible soluti
other connection(s); use the server mode [90020-197]
```

Figure 26. The database may be already in use exception

The first step is to define the new **Postgres** database to move to:

```
D:\setup>set MB_JETTY_PORT=3001

D:\setup>set MB_DB_TYPE=postgres

D:\setup>set MB_DB_NAME=metabase

D:\setup>set MB_DB_PORT=5432

D:\setup>set MB_DB_USER=metabase

D:\setup>set MB_DB_PASS=123456

D:\setup>set MB_DB_HOST=localhost
```

The second step is to do the migration with below command:

```
D:\setup>java -jar metabase.0.37.6.jar load-from-h2 ./metabase.db
```

Please do not add suffixes like **.h2.db** or **mv.db** into the command

Figure 27. The H2 database files in the system

You will see something like this:

```
2021-03-05 13:48:57,608 INFO db.liquibase :: Database has unrun migrations. Waiti
ock to be cleared...
2021-03-05 13:48:57,627 INFO db.liquibase :: Migration lock is cleared. Running n
2021-03-05 13:48:57,685 INFO metabase.db :: Database Migrations Current ...
Database setup took 4.1 s
Testing if target DB is already populated...
←[32m[OK]←[0m
Temporarily disabling DB constraints...
←[32m[OK]←[0m
Transfering 1 instances of Database...←[34m.←[0m←[32m[OK]←[0m
```

```
Transfering 13 instances of DataMigrations...←[34m.←[0m←[32m[OK]←[0m
Re-enabling DB constraints...
←[32m[OK]←[0m
Setting postgres sequence ids to proper values...
```

Now restart the **Metabase** on the same terminal to keep the environment variables and check again on the web UI:

```
D:\setup>java -jar metabase.0.37.6.jar
```

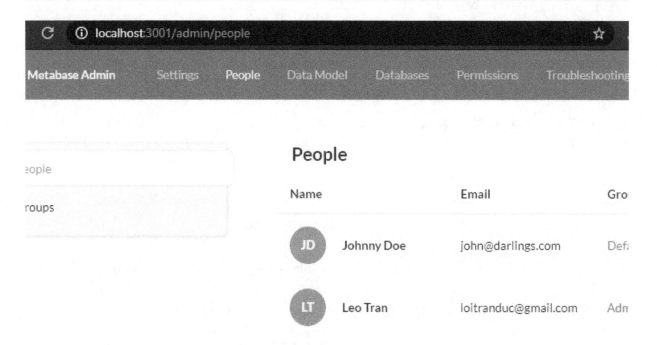

Figure 28. The Metabase UI after migrating

We can see the Johnny Doe user on the new **Metabase**.

> Please note that you can't use a populated **Postgres** database (the database that already has another **Metabase** data inside) to migrate to. You need to clean the database before migration.
>
> The migration error will be something like this:

```
Database setup took 5.5 s
Testing if target DB is already populated...
java.lang.AssertionError: Assert failed: Target DB is already populated!
(not (mb-db-populated? target-db-conn))
        at metabase.cmd.load_from_h2$load_from_h2_BANG_$fn__73958.invoke(load_from_h2.
        at clojure.java.jdbc$db_transaction_STAR_.invokeStatic(jdbc.clj:807)
        at clojure.java.jdbc$db_transaction_STAR_.invoke(jdbc.clj:776)
        at clojure.java.jdbc$db_transaction_STAR_.invokeStatic(jdbc.clj:852)
        at clojure.java.jdbc$db_transaction_STAR_.invoke(jdbc.clj:776)


        at metabase.core$_main.invokeStatic(core.clj:172)
        at metabase.core$_main.doInvoke(core.clj:167)
        at clojure.lang.RestFn.applyTo(RestFn.java:137)
        at metabase.core.main(Unknown Source)
Command failed with exception: Assert failed: Target DB is already populated!
(not (mb-db-populated? target-db-conn))
```

Figure 29. Target DB is already populated exception

1.3. References

- https://www.metabase.com/docs
- https://github.com/Markenson/csv-metabase-driver
- https://www.metabase.com/docs/latest/operations-guide/migrating-from-h2.html

Chapter 2: Adding Data Sources

In the previous chapter, you have done installing a **Metabase**. In this chapter, we will add various kinds of data sources: **CSV** files, **MySQL**, **Oracle** database ….

2.1. Adding a CSV data source

In previous chapter, we have the CSV driver installed on Metabase. In this section, we will add a sample **CSV** data source to use in **Metabase**.

First of all, I have placed sample **CSV** files at **metabase101/chapter02/csv**:

Figure 30. CSV Files on the repository

Metabase allows you to gather multiples CSV files in a single folder to form a data source. Each single CSV file can be considered as a table as in other relational databases like **Oracle**, **MySQL**...

Importing CSV files from local disks

Now we will add a new data source from CSV files in local disks. I have 3 files on my local disk:

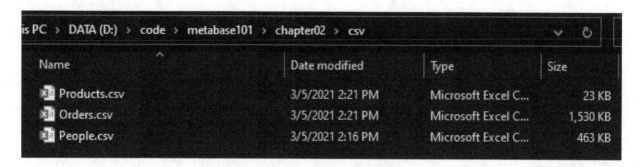

Figure 31. CSV files on local disks

Go to menu **Admin -> Database -> Add Database**:

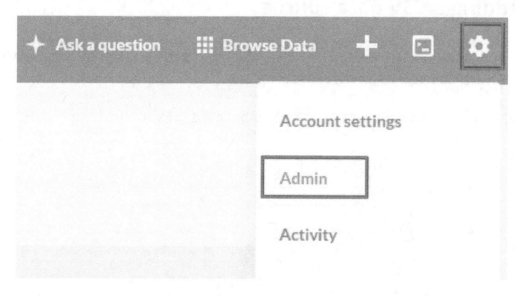

Figure 32. The Metabase's admin menu

Figure 33. Adding a new database

Now select Database type as **CSV** and fill the form like the image below:

Figure 34. Adding local CSV files into Metabase

Save the configuration, and you can see that you have had the **SampleCSV** data source on the Database page. Now go back to the **Data Model** page and check the newly added **SampleCSV** database.

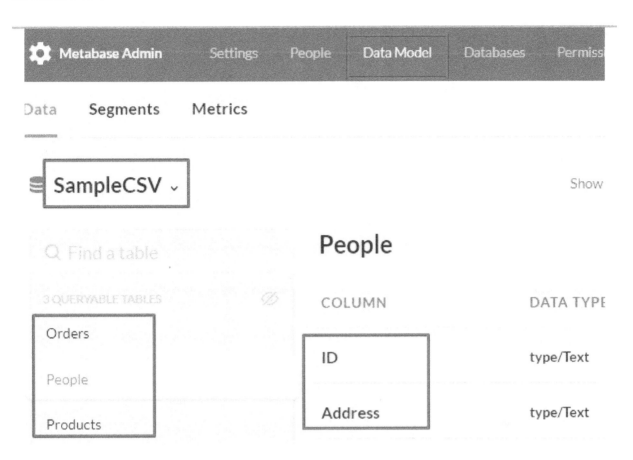

Figure 35. Browsing the CSV data model

Importing CSV files from a Github repository

The **CSV** driver has the ability to import **CSV** files directly from a Github repository which is a pretty handful as you don't have to download **CSV** files into your local machine.

Go back to menu **Database -> Add Database** and choose CSV type with following configuration:

- **Name**: *RemoteCSV*
- **Filename**: *https://raw.githubusercontent.com/loitd/metabase101/main/chapter02/csv/*
- **Separator**: *,*
- **Charset**: *utf-8*
- **Advanced**: *&quotechar=&customTableList=Orders,People,Products*

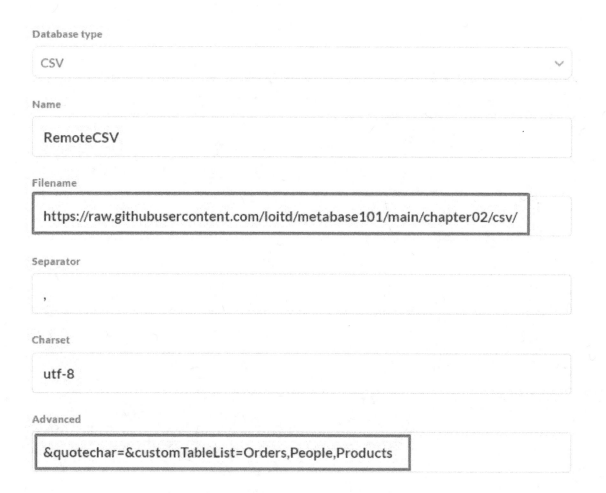

Figure 36. Adding CSV files from remote github

Please note that you have to define the **customTableList** parameter as in the above image. A dialog showed up to notify that the database is added.

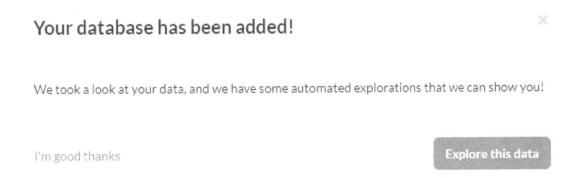

Figure 37. The adding database dialog

Check again on the **Data Model** page:

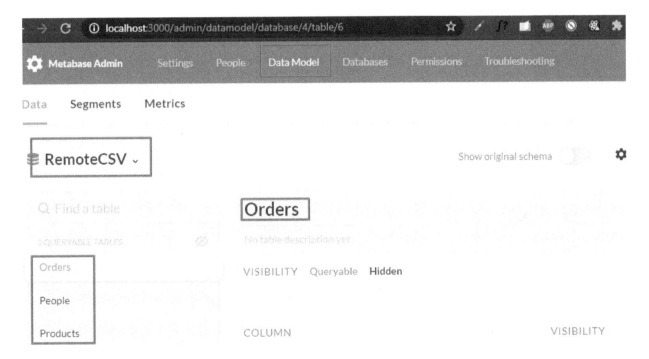

Figure 38. The RemoteCSV from Github on the Data Model menu

2.2. Adding a MySQL data source

We will add a **MySQL** data source to our existing **Metabase**.

Preparing a MySQL database

First of all, we will create a new **MySQL** database user named **metabase101** for the **Metabase** using the script at **metabase101/chapter02/2.2/CreateMySQLUser.sql**:

```
CREATE USER 'metabase101'@'%' IDENTIFIED VIA mysql_native_password USING
'your-secured-password';

GRANT USAGE ON *.* TO 'metabase101'@'%' REQUIRE NONE WITH
MAX_QUERIES_PER_HOUR 0 MAX_CONNECTIONS_PER_HOUR 0 MAX_UPDATES_PER_HOUR 0
MAX_USER_CONNECTIONS 0;

CREATE DATABASE IF NOT EXISTS `metabase101`;

GRANT ALL PRIVILEGES ON `metabase101`.* TO 'metabase101'@'%';

GRANT ALL PRIVILEGES ON `metabase101\_%`.* TO 'metabase101'@'%';
```

You can find the script in the book's Github repository.

Test your login with your MySQL manager. I am using **HeidiSQL**:

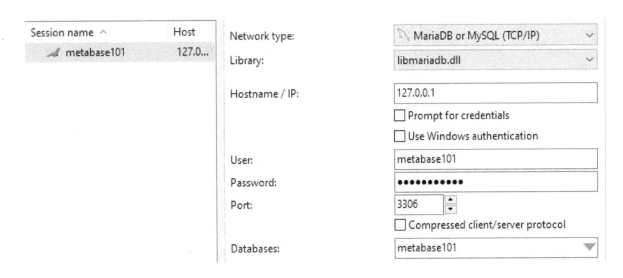

Figure 39. Logging in MySQL with MySQL manager

Create table **ORDERS** with the script at
metabase101/chapter02/2.2/CreateTables.sql.

Insert the test data into table **ORDERS** with the script at
`metabase101/chapter02/2.2/InsertQuery.sql`.

Browse your data in the MySQL database:

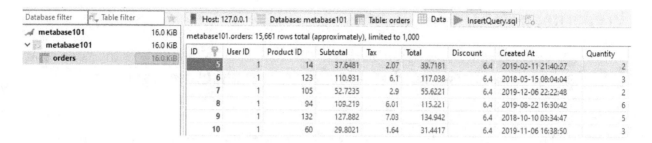

Figure 40. Browsing data in the MySQL database

Connecting to the MySQL database

Go back to **Admin** > **Database** and add a new database

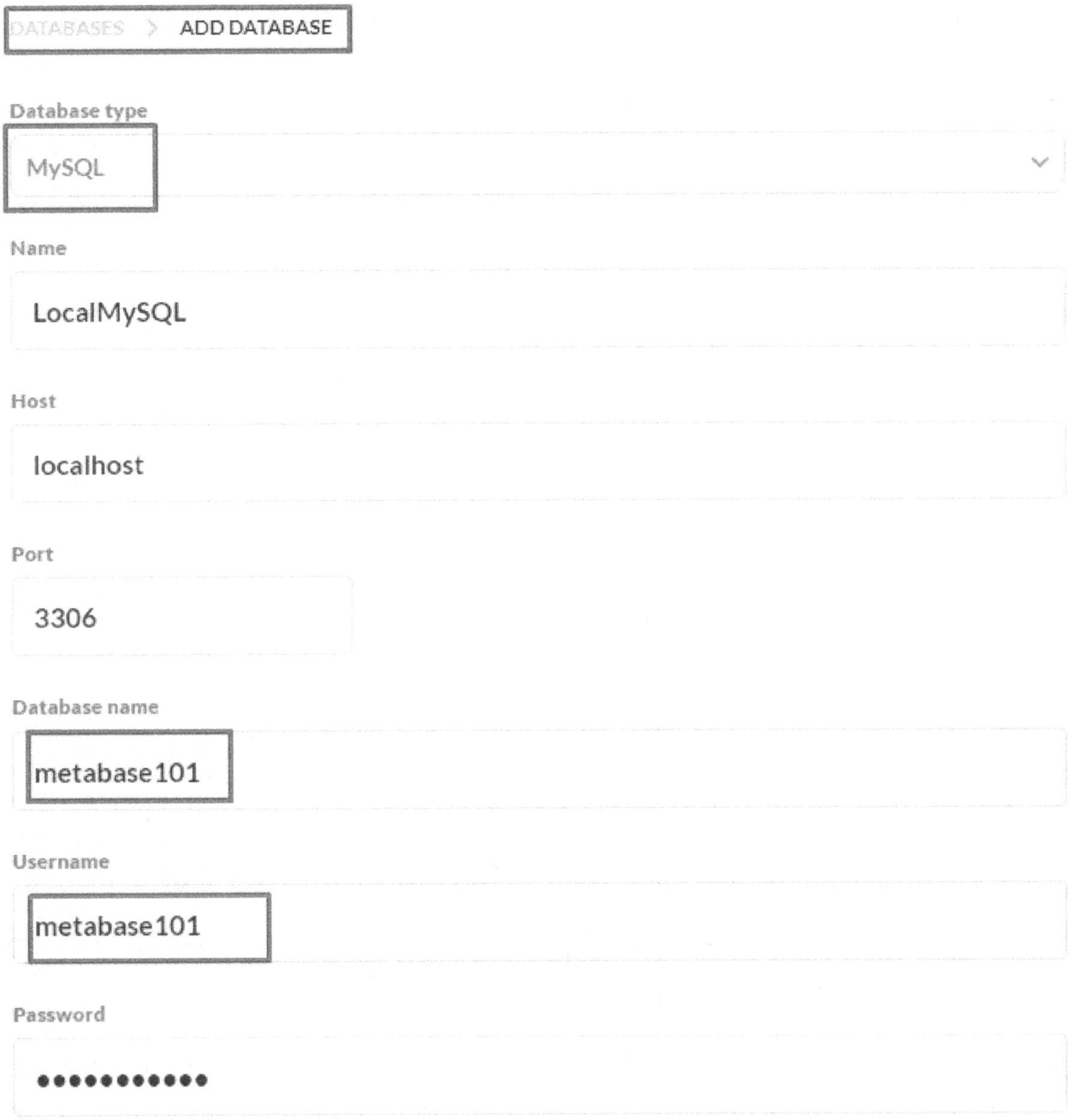

Figure 41. Adding a new MySQL database

Check again on the **Data Model** page:

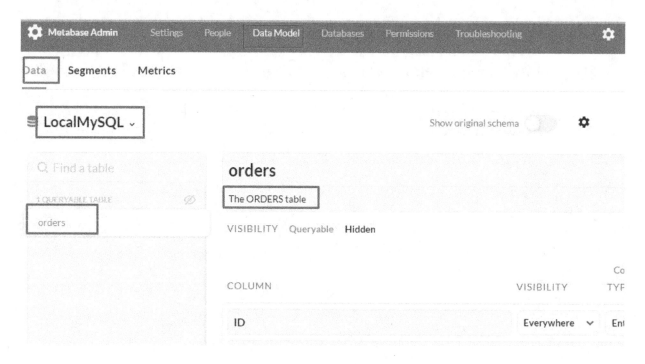

Figure 42. Checking the data on the Data Model page

2.3. Adding an Oracle data source

Like adding a MySQL database in the previous section, go to **Admin > Databases** and click the **Add database** button

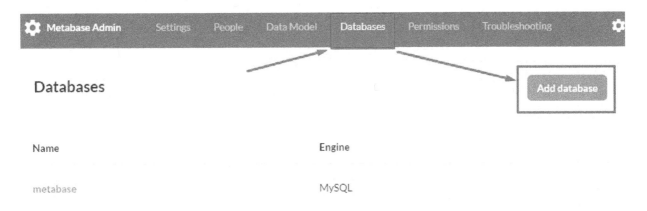

Figure 43. Adding a new database

Fill in the form as an example below:

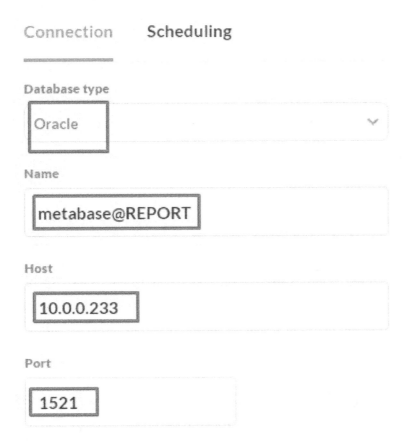

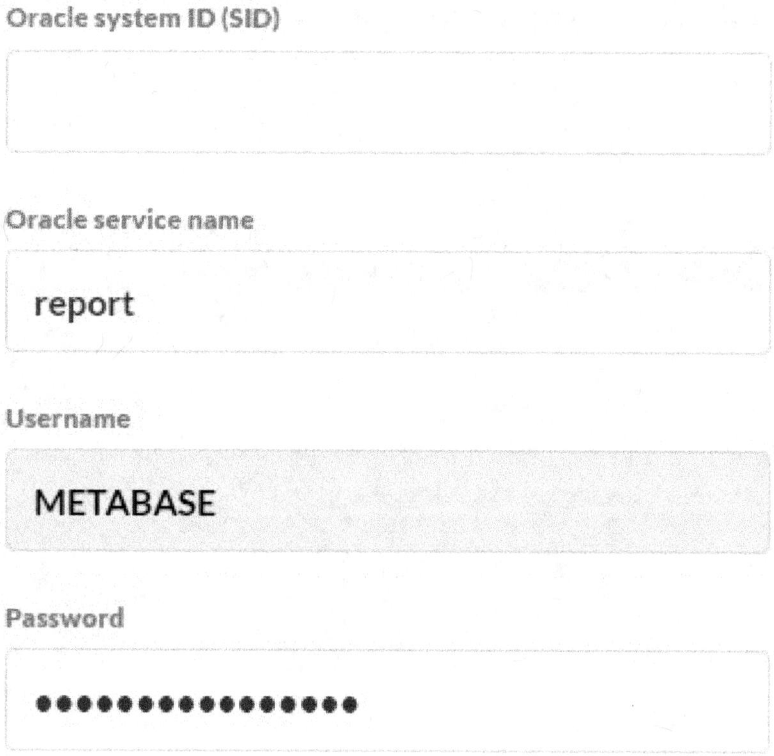

Oracle system ID (SID)

Oracle service name

report

Username

METABASE

Password

●●●●●●●●●●●●●●●●●

Use an SSH-tunnel for database connections

Some database installations can only be accessed
by connecting through an SSH bastion host. This
option also provides an extra layer of security
when a VPN is not available. Enabling this is
usually slower than a direct connection.

**Automatically run queries when doing simple
filtering and summarizing**

When this is on, Metabase will automatically run
queries when users do simple explorations with
the Summarize and Filter buttons when viewing
a table or chart. You can turn this off if querying
this database is slow. This setting doesn't affect
drill-throughs or SQL queries.

**This is a large database, so let me choose when
Metabase syncs and scans**

By default, Metabase does a lightweight hourly
sync and an intensive daily scan of field values. If
you have a large database, we recommend
turning this on and reviewing when and how
often the field value scans happen.

Figure 44. Filling in the tab Connection of the form

I suggest you choose the option to turn off database syncing in case you have a large database
especially when it is a transactional database.

By default, **Metabase** will do a database syncing job hourly to check for updates to the
database's schema. Switch to tab **Scheduling** to see these configurations:

Database syncing

This is a lightweight process that checks for updates to this database's schema. In most cases, you should be fine leaving this set to sync hourly.

Scanning for Filter Values

Metabase can scan the values present in each field in this database to enable checkbox filters in dashboards and questions. This can be a somewhat resource-intensive process, particularly if you have a very large database. When should Metabase automatically scan and cache field values?

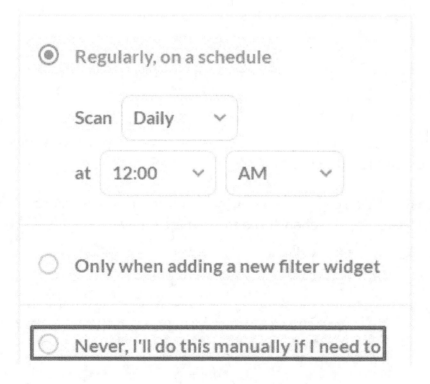

Figure 45. Scheduling for the database

2.5. References

- https://metabase.com/docs
- https://github.com/Markenson/csv-metabase-driver

Chapter 3: Basic Configurations

In the previous chapter, you've learned how to add new data sources to **Metabase**. In this chapter, we will work through additional configurations needed for the **Metabase**. Authentication using **LDAP**, `Google Authentication`, email, `Slack`, and some fine-tuning configurations to help **Metabase** more secured.

3.1. Authentication

There are several kinds of authentication methods supported by **Metabase**. They are:

- Google Authentication
- LDAP
- Manually created by the administrator

LDAP Configuration

First choose the **LDAP** configuration from `Admin > Settings > Authentication`

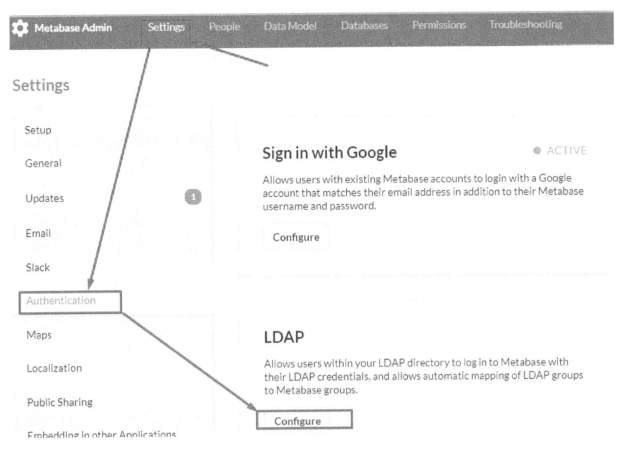

Figure 46. The LDAP configuration

Take a look at the below sample configuration:

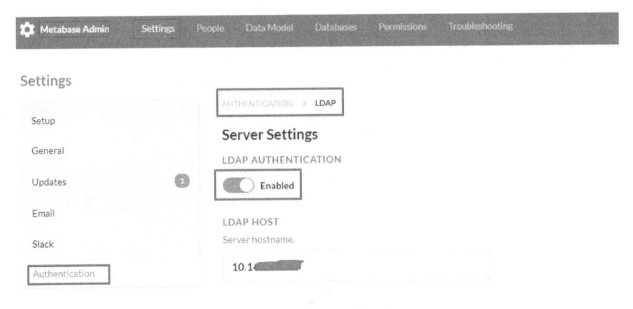

Figure 47. LDAP Host configuration

Your DN may look like this:

`CN=metabase,CN=Users,DC=leotrancorp,DC=vn`

Embedding in other Applications

Caching

LDAP SECURITY

None   **SSL**   **StartTLS**

USERNAME OR DN

The Distinguished Name to bind as (if any), this user will be used to lookup information about othe users.

> CN=metabase,CN=Users,DC=▓▓▓▓▓▓,DC=vn

PASSWORD

The password to bind with for the lookup user.

> ●●●●●●●●●●●●

Figure 48. DN Setting

Set `USER FILTER = (|(sAMAccountName={login})(userPrincipalName={login}))`.

User Schema

USER SEARCH BASE

Search base for users. (Will be searched recursively)

> DC=▓▓▓▓▓▓,DC=vn

USER FILTER

User lookup filter, the placeholder {login} will be replaced by the user supplied login.

> (|(sAMAccountName={login})(userPrincipalName={lc

▼ **Attributes**

EMAIL ATTRIBUTE

Attribute to use for the users email. (usually 'mail', 'email' or 'userPrincipalName')

> userprincipalname

FIRST NAME ATTRIBUTE

Attribute to use for the user's first name. (usually 'givenName')

> givenname

LAST NAME ATTRIBUTE

Attribute to use for the user's last name. (usually 'sn')

> samaccountname

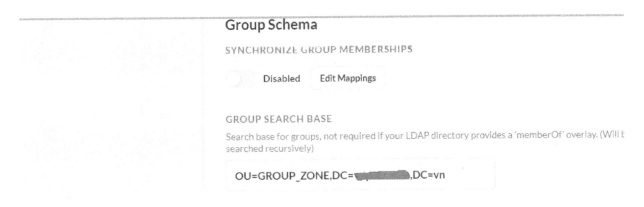

Figure 49. Set user and group schema

Go to **Admin > People** to see all LDAP logged in account has a gray icon as in the image below:

Figure 50. A LDAP user with additional icon

Google Authentication

First of all, login to your **Google Cloud Console** and create a new project at:
https://console.cloud.google.com/projectcreate?previousPage=%2Fprojectselector2%2Fapis%2Fcredentials%3Fpli%3D1%26supportedpurview%3Dproject&supportedpurview=project

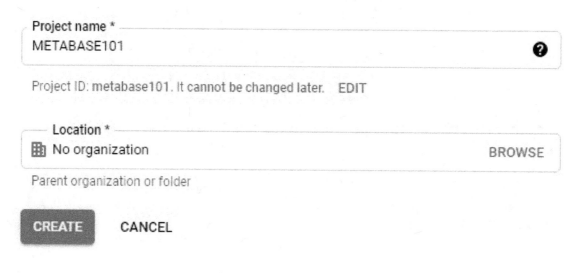

Figure 51. Google cloud console

Now you will be redirected to the **Credentials** page

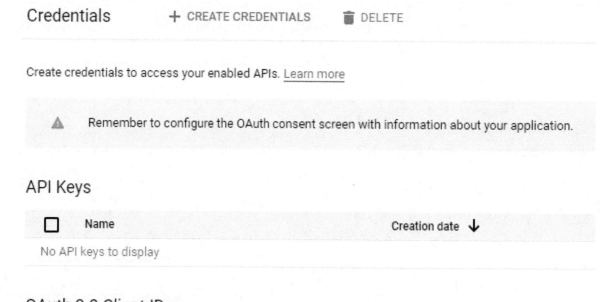

Figure 52. Creating credentials

Create a new Oauth Client ID:

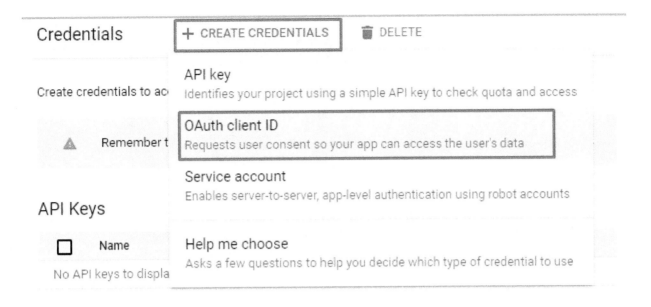

Figure 53. Creating new Oauth client ID

Google asks to complete the **Consent Screen** first

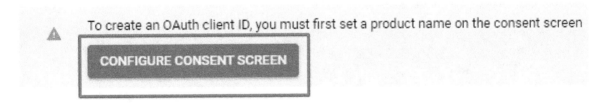

← Create OAuth client ID

A client ID is used to identify a single app to Google's OAuth servers. If your app runs on multiple platforms, each will need its own client ID. See Setting up OAuth 2.0 for more information.

⚠   To create an OAuth client ID, you must first set a product name on the consent screen

CONFIGURE CONSENT SCREEN

Figure 54. Configure the consent screen

Now select the scope of consent:

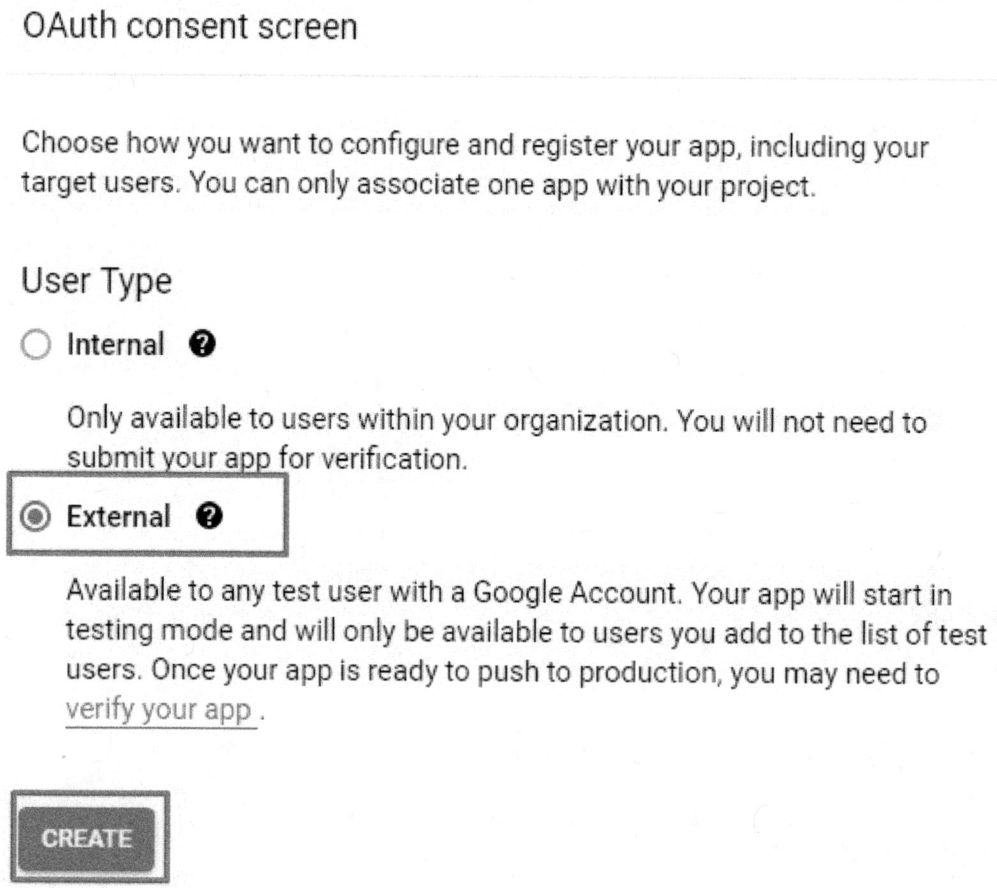

OAuth consent screen

Choose how you want to configure and register your app, including your target users. You can only associate one app with your project.

User Type

○ Internal

Only available to users within your organization. You will not need to submit your app for verification.

◉ External

Available to any test user with a Google Account. Your app will start in testing mode and will only be available to users you add to the list of test users. Once your app is ready to push to production, you may need to verify your app .

CREATE

Figure 55. Set user type to be External

Now fill in the application information:

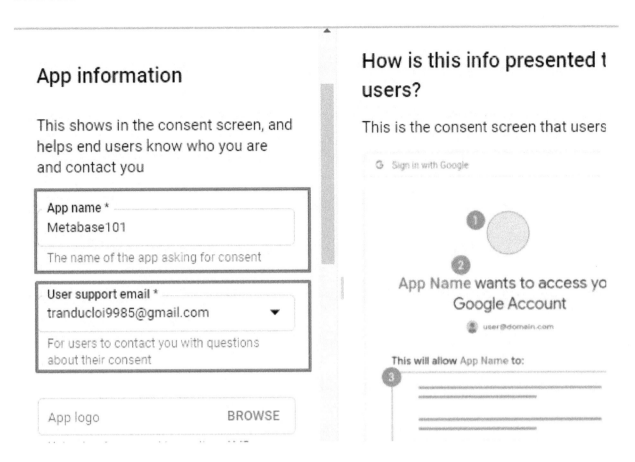

Figure 56. Filling in the app information

Fill in the application domain:

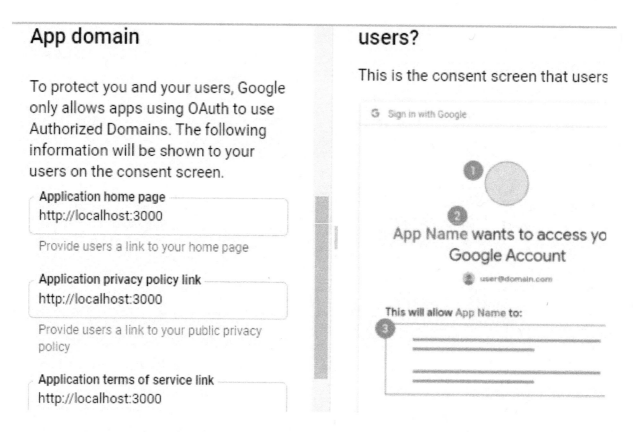

Figure 57. Filling the app domain

At the end of the page, fill in the developer contact:

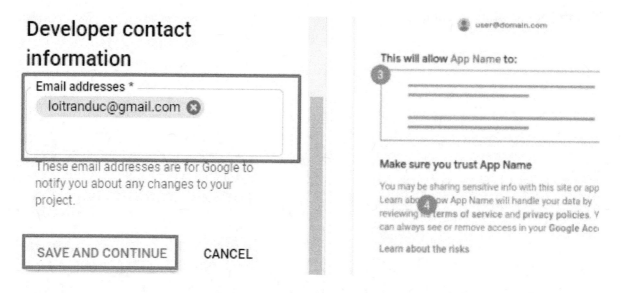

Figure 58. Filling in the developer contact

Press **Save and Continue**, you will be redirected to the select scope page:

Edit app registration

Scopes express the permissions you request users to authorize for your app and allow your project to access specific types of private user data from their Google Account. Learn more

Figure 59. Editing app registration

Tick the below permission scopes that your application need

Figure 60. Choosing the permission scopes

Save and continue to add test users to your app:

Test users

While publishing status is set to "Testing", only test users are able to access the app. Allowed user cap prior to app verification is 100, and is counted over the entire lifetime of the app. Learn more

+ ADD USERS

Figure 61. Adding test users

Add your desired users that can access the application even when it has not been published yet. Finally, press **Back to Dashboard**. You will be forwarded to the Consent Screen home page.

OAuth consent screen

Metabase101   ✏️ EDIT APP

Publishing status ❓

Testing

PUBLISH APP

Figure 62. Checking publishing status

Now go back to the **Create Oauth Client ID** page

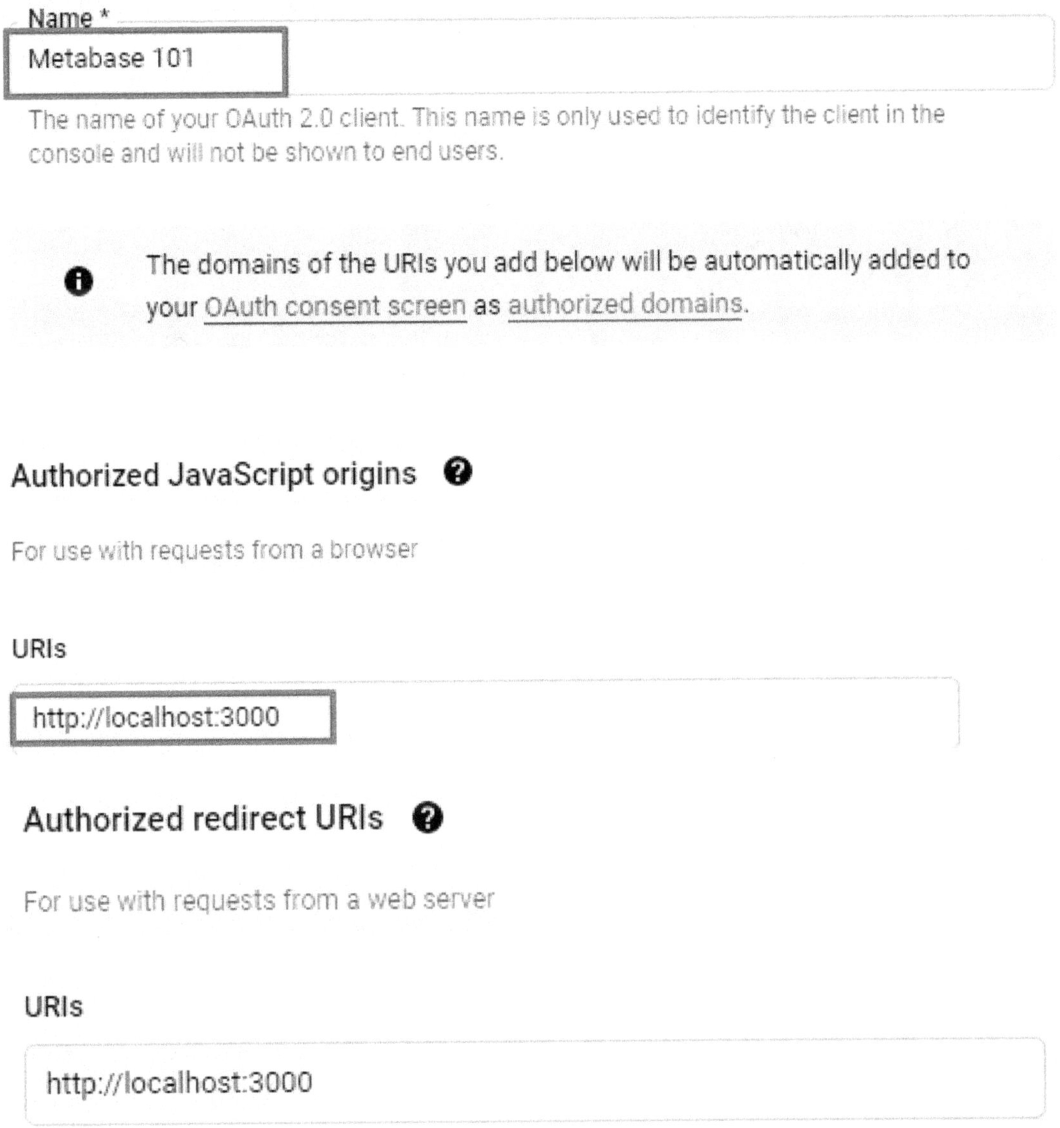

Name *
Metabase 101
The name of your OAuth 2.0 client. This name is only used to identify the client in the console and will not be shown to end users.
The domains of the URIs you add below will be automatically added to your OAuth consent screen as authorized domains.
Authorized JavaScript origins
For use with requests from a browser
URIs
http://localhost:3000
Authorized redirect URIs
For use with requests from a web server
URIs
http://localhost:3000

Figure 63. Set the URIs

There will be a dialog to show your newly created credentials

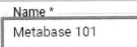

OAuth client created

The client ID and secret can always be accessed from Credentials in APIs & Services

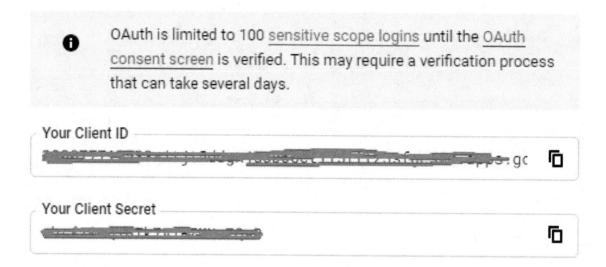

Figure 64. Viewing client ID and secret

Now go back to the **Metabase** and add the **Google Authentication** setting:

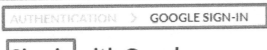

Sign in with Google

Allows users with existing Metabase accounts to login with a Google account that matches their email address in addition to their Metabase username and password.

To allow users to sign in with Google you'll need to give Metabase a Google Developers console application client ID. It only takes a few steps and instructions on how to create a key can be found here.

Be sure to include the full client ID, including the apps.googleusercontent.com suffix.

Allow users to sign up on their own if their Google account email address is from:

@   gmail.com

Figure 65. Setting the Google Sign-in in Metabase

This may be the most important part of this section. First of all, you need to fill in your application's client ID to allow users who have the Google account can log in. To allow whoever has a Gmail account be able to `sign up`, fill `gmail.com` into the second textbox.

Log out current session, you will have a **Login with Google** button on your screen:

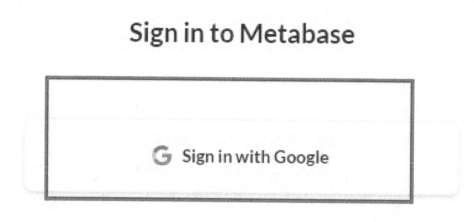

Figure 66. Sign-in with Google button

Click the `Sign in with Google` button, you will be logged in. Sign out and log in with the admin account to check the user list

Figure 67. Logged in with the Google authentication

You see that the user has the **Google** logo next to their email. Please note that users created with Google Sign-in do not have their password created and must use Google to log in our **Metabase**.

3.2. Email Configuration

First, we will create a **Google** application password according to this help:

gle Account Help   Q   Describe your issue

Create & use App Passwords

If you use 2-Step-Verification and get a "password incorrect" error when you sign in, you can try to use an App Password.

1. Go to your Google Account ☑ .
2. Select **Security**.
3. Under "Signing in to Google," select **App Passwords**. You may need to sign in. If you don't have this option, it might be because:
   a. 2-Step Verification is not set up for your account.
   b. 2-Step Verification is only set up for security keys.
   c. Your account is through work, school, or other organization.
   d. You turned on Advanced Protection.
4. At the bottom, choose **Select app** and choose the app you using > **Select device** and choose the device you're using > **Generate**.
5. Follow the instructions to enter the App Password. The App Password is the 16-character code in the yellow bar on your device.
6. Tap **Done**.

Tip: Most of the time, you'll only have to enter an App Password once per app or device, so don't worry about memorizing it.

Figure 68. How to access Google app password from official Google support

79

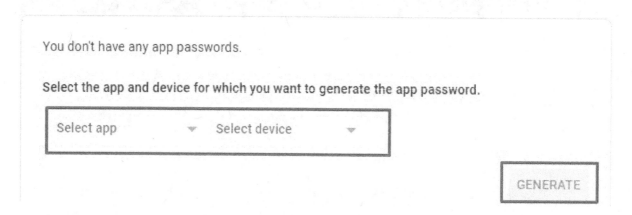

Figure 69. Configure Google app passwords

Now configure the email for your **Metabase** by accessing https://your-metabase-server:port/admin/settings/email

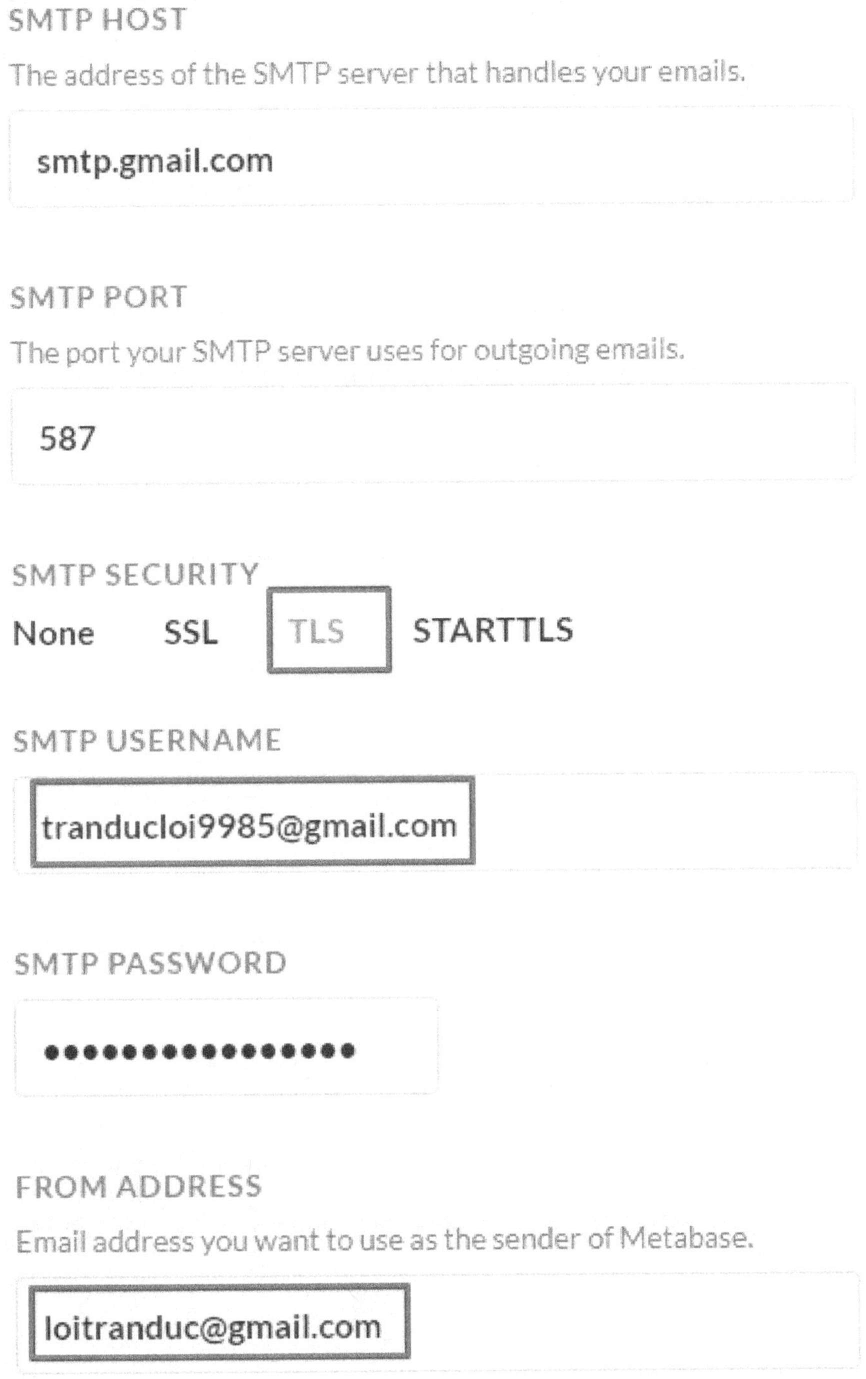

SMTP HOST

The address of the SMTP server that handles your emails.

smtp.gmail.com

SMTP PORT

The port your SMTP server uses for outgoing emails.

587

SMTP SECURITY

None   SSL   TLS   STARTTLS

SMTP USERNAME

tranducloi9985@gmail.com

SMTP PASSWORD

●●●●●●●●●●●●●●●●●

FROM ADDRESS

Email address you want to use as the sender of Metabase.

loitranduc@gmail.com

Figure 70. The Email configuration in Metabase

Press **Send Test Mail** button to test your configuration

Figure 71. Sending a test email

Check your mailbox for the sent test email.

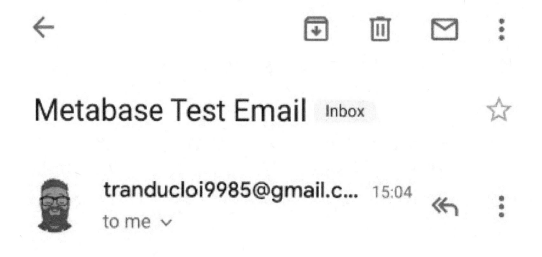

Figure 72. Checking the Metabase's test email

3.3. Slack Configuration

Metabase allows us to send alerts to our Slack channel. In order to do that, we need to access your Slack workspace first. You may need to create a new one if you haven't had anyone yet.

Workspaces for **tranducloi9985@gmail.com**

LeoTran Inc.
0 members   →

Figure 73. Create new account and workspace

Create a new channel named **metabase_files**:

Figure 74. Create new channel

Now in the Slack workspace, create a new Slack bot

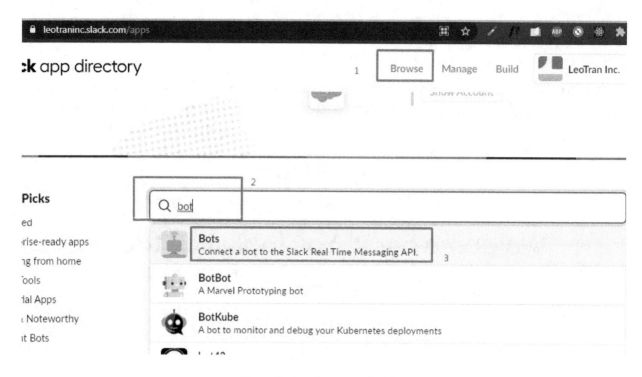

Figure 75. Creating a new Slack bot

Now press the **Add to Slack** button

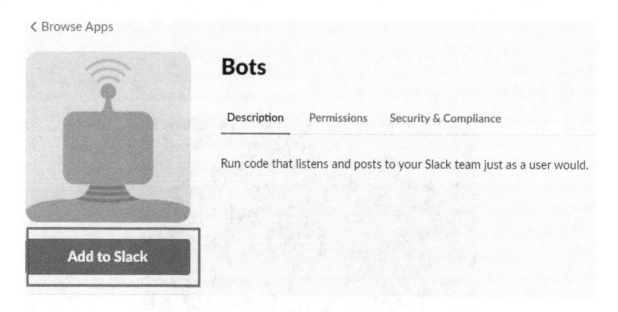

Figure 76. Add the bot to Slack

Now fill in the name for your new bot:

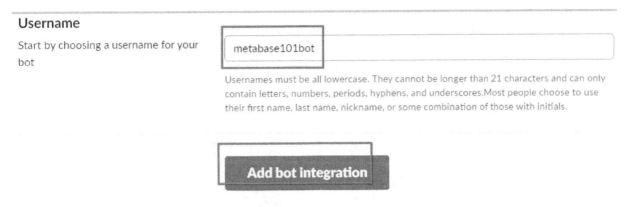

Figure 77. Configuring the bot

Now you will be forwarded to bot configuration page:

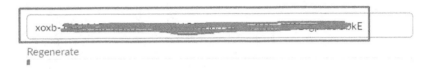

Figure 78. The Slack bot token page

Copy the API Token and go back to the **Metabase's** setting page

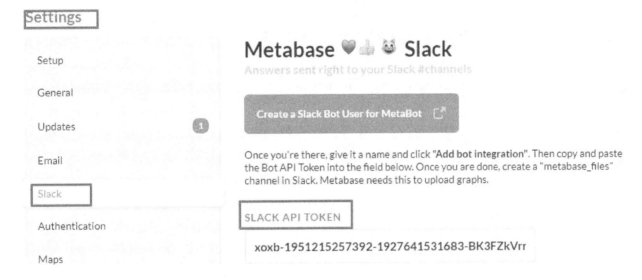

Figure 79. Configuring the Metabase Slack token

Paste your Slack API Token the save your changes and you are done. The **Metabase** messages in a Slack channel look like this:

Figure 80. A sample Metabase message to a Slack channel

3.4. Some additional configurations

There are some additional configurations you may need to adjust **Metabase** to suit your need.

Disable Friendly Table and Field Names

Go to **Setting** > **General**

FRIENDLY TABLE AND FIELD NAMES

Metabase can attempt to transform your table and field names into more sensible, human-readable versions, e.g. "somehorriblename" becomes "Some Horrible Name". This doesn't work all that well if the names are in a language other than English, however. Do you want us to take a guess?

Figure 81. Disable friendly table and field names

Modify Report Timezone

Go to **Setting** > **General**

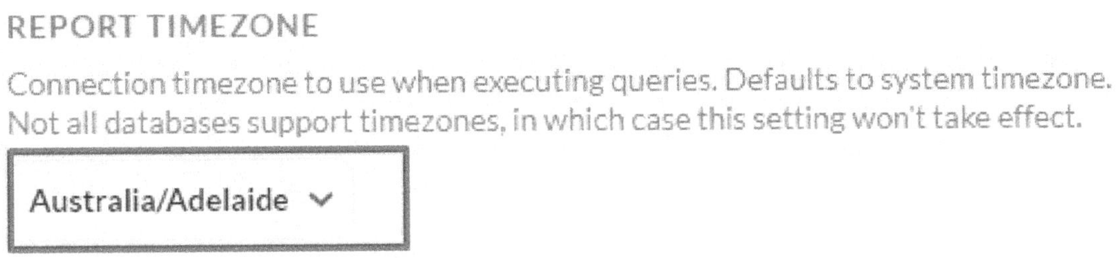

REPORT TIMEZONE

Connection timezone to use when executing queries. Defaults to system timezone.
Not all databases support timezones, in which case this setting won't take effect.

Australia/Adelaide ∨

Figure 82. Report time zone

Modify The First Day of The Week

Go to **`Setting`** > **`Localization`**

FIRST DAY OF THE WEEK
This will affect things like grouping by week or filtering in GUI queries. It won't affect SQL queries.
Monday

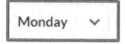

Figure 83. The first day of the week

Revoking all default permissions

By default, newly created users will be assign a default role with default access to all data sources (which is too risky in my opinion), so we should change these default settings.

Figure 84. Revoking the default permissions

In the **All Users** column, press **Data Access** for each data source and choose **Revoke**

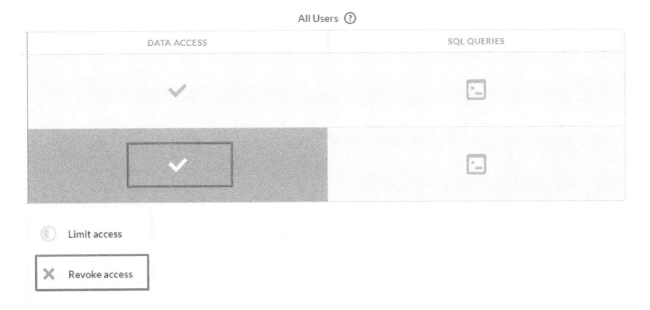

Figure 85. Revoking user permissions (cont)

Continue until all permissions for **All Users** have been revoked.

Figure 86. Revoking user permissions (cont)

3.5. References

- https://www.metabase.com/docs/latest/administration-guide/10-single-sign-on.html

Chapter 4: Users, Groups, and Permissions

In the previous chapter, you have learned how to set up a complete **Metabase** system with a lot of configurations. In chapter 4 and chapter 5, based on the company's hierarchy, we will organize the report for the whole company. You will be guided to create users, groups, permissions, analytics, collections, and reports based on the pre-defined hierarchy. At the end of Chapter 5, you will know how the whole **Metabase** reporting system works.

4.1. The company structure

I have created a sample basic company hierarchy as below:

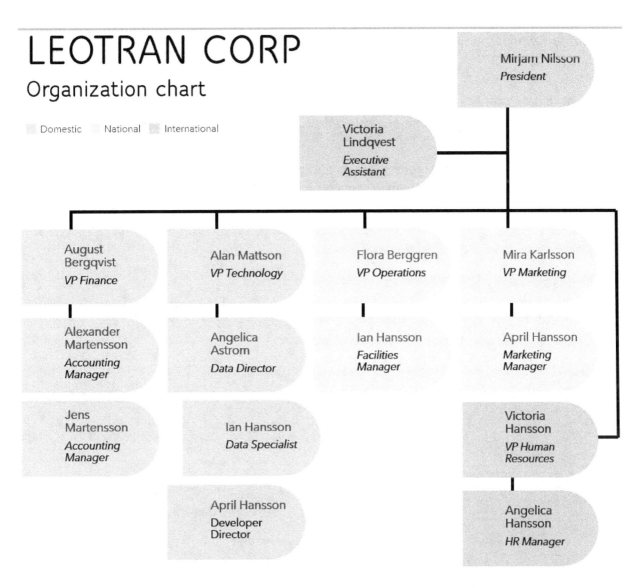

Figure 87. The LeoTran Corp organization chart

This type of chart is very common, your company may need a little modification or at the beginning, your boss may want you to apply to a part of the company (instead of applying to the whole company). But in general, this structure can be applied to most kinds of companies.

Now we need to define our **rule of permissions**:

- Everyone has a separate account.
- President and Executive Assistant can **view** all reports.
- VP can view all reports belong to their section e.g., VP Finance can view all financial reports.
- Data Director is a **Metabase** administrator.
- Data Specialists can access and write raw SQL on all databases.

Without those rules, no permission scheme can be made. Our users and permissions will go unmanageable.

When there is any confirmed exception, you need to modify the rules. You need to keep the rule as clean as possible so anyone at any level can read and understand easily.

 During this process, you should have a copy of our rule of permissions beside. All processes in chapter 4 and chapter 5 are based totally on those rules.

4.2. Creating user accounts

According to rule number one, "**Everyone has a separate account**", we need to create new accounts for all users. You can ignore this part if you have configured:

- LDAP authentication AND/OR
- Google Authentication

As I have mentioned in Chapter 3.1: Authentication, users can register and log themselves in without any prevention from the administrators. If you haven't done any of them, you need to create accounts manually (as below).

Go to the **People** page

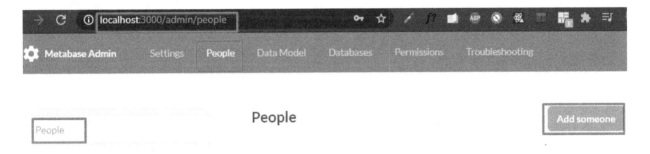

Figure 88. Add a new person

Click the **Add someone** button

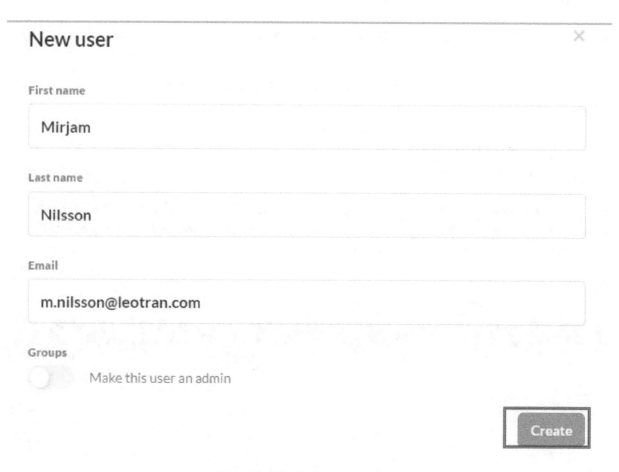

Figure 89. Filling in the new user form

A dialog will be shown to let us know we have added successfully.

Figure 90. The new user dialog

In **Metabase**, new users will be automatically in the **Default** group. Continue to add all remaining users. We will change the user's group later.

4.3. Creating groups

Metabase doesn't use the role concept, instead of that, it uses **Groups** to categorize users and permissions. In my opinion, they work the same under the hood.

Look back to the LeoTran Corp organization chart, we need to create a group for each role on the chart. We have roles listed below:

- President
- Execute Assistant
- VP Finance
- Accounting Manager
- VP Technology
- Data Director
- Data Specialist
- Developer Director
- VP Operation
- Facilities Manager
- VP Marketing
- Marketing Manager
- VP Human Resources
- HR Manager

We simply create each role an equivalent group manually. First, we go to **Admin** > **People** > **Group** and press the **Create a group** button.

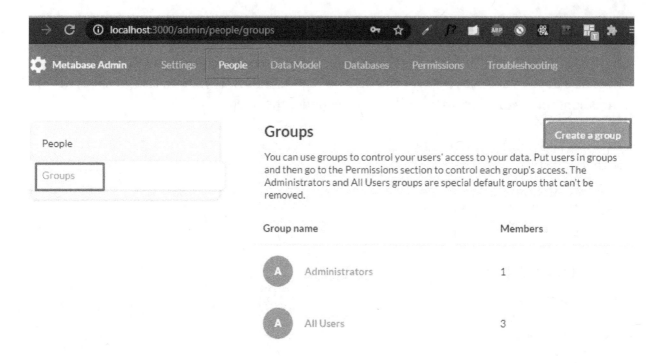

Figure 91. Creating a new group

As you can see, by default, **Metabase** creates **Administrators** and **All Users** groups. A user can belong to as many groups as possible. You can't modify the **All Users** group even when you are an administrator.

 The **Administrators** group always has the highest level in the **Metabase** system.

Everyone belongs to the **All Users** group, you can't modify this group (e.g. change the group name, add members, remove members).

Make sure to revoke all permissions of the **All Users** group to secure your **Metabase**.

Now fill in the desired group name and press the **Add** button

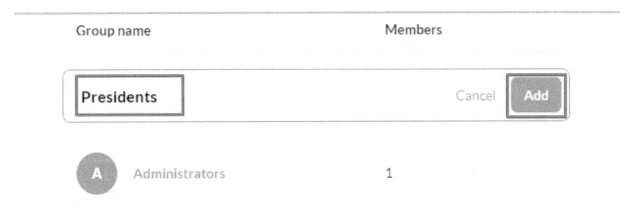

Figure 92. Adding a desired group

Continue to add all remaining groups. In case you want to change the name of an existing group, press the triple-dot button beside the group name.

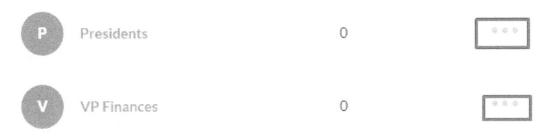

Figure 93. Changing the name of an existing group

Choose the **Edit Name** or **Remove Group** button

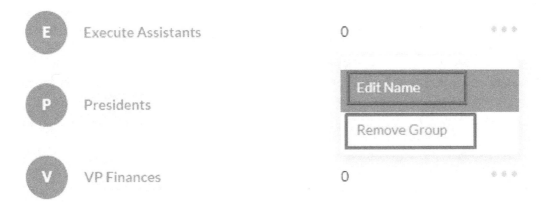

Figure 94. Editing an existing group

4.4. Adding users into groups

This process aims to assign roles to user accounts. Later, we shall map permissions to groups. In any case, you shouldn't try to map permissions directly to user accounts, not only in **Metabase** but also in all kinds of **Role-Base-Access-Control (RBAC)** models.

In the groups setting page, click the **Groups** link:

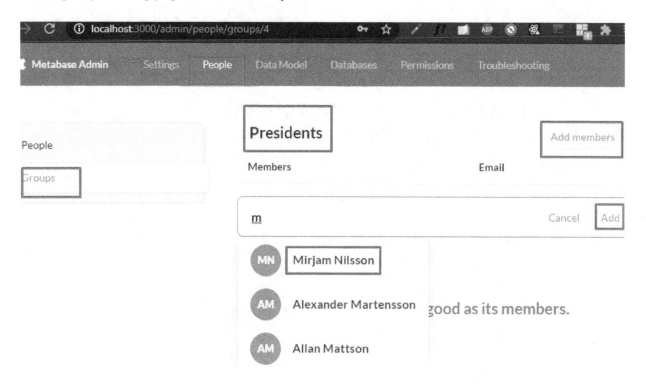

Figure 95. Adding a user to the group

Now press the **Add members** button and type the name of the user you want to add to the group, **Metabase** will search and display the list of users in a drop-down list as you type. Continue to add other users to the group based on the organization chart in section 4.1.

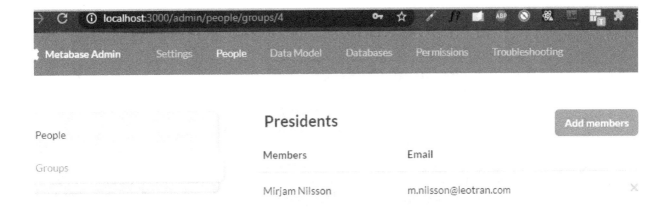

Figure 96. People added to the group

Refresh the group setting page, you will see the number of members in each group displayed beside the group names.

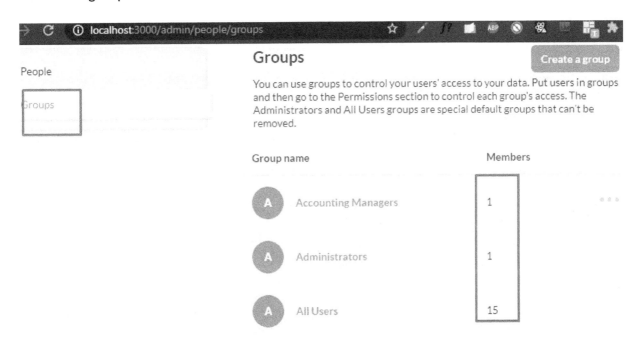

Figure 97. Members counted in groups

4.5. Setting up group permissions

Revoking All Users group permissions

We will revoke all permissions belonging to the **All Users** group. First, go to **Admin** > **Permissions** > **Data permissions**

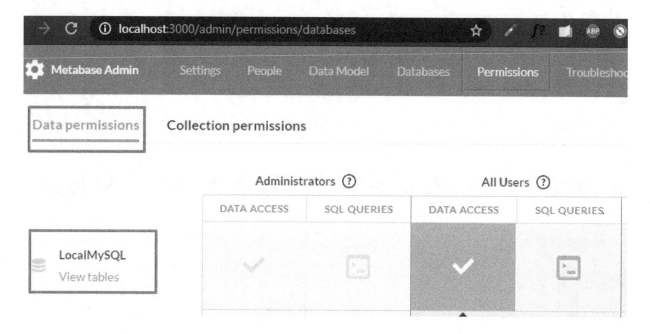

Figure 98. List of permissions for databases

Click **Data Access** and choose **Revoke Access**

Data permissions   **Collection permissions**

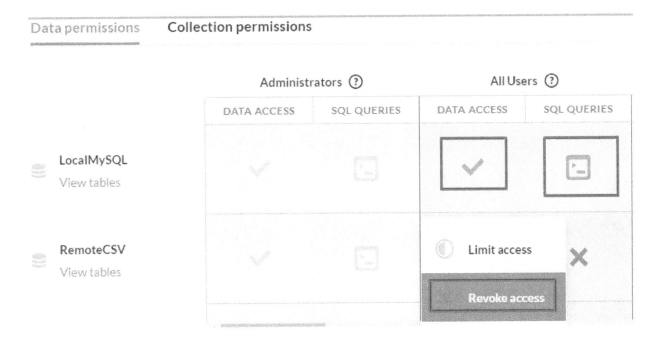

Figure 99. Revoking access from the All Users group

Your **All Users** group will look like this

Figure 100. Permissions revoked

Press the **Save Changes** button at the right top corner

Figure 101. Saving the changes

Confirm the changes

Save permissions?

All Users will be denied access to 1 table in LocalMySQL.
All Users will no longer be able to read or write native queries for LocalMySQL.

Are you sure you want to do this?

Cancel

Figure 102. Confirming the changes dialog

Setting the Data Director permissions

Now, according to our rule of permissions in section 4.1, we need to set the Data Director to be a **Metabase** Administrator.

Go to **Admin > People** then find user **Angelica Astrom** who belongs to the **Data Directors** group then press the triple-dot button.

Figure 103. Editing a user

Choose **Edit User** in the drop-down menu:

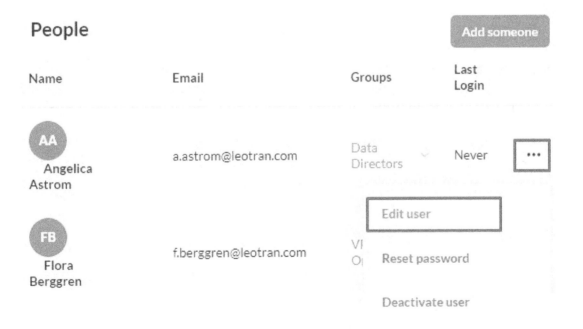

Figure 104. Editing a user (cont)

Now check to add this user to the **Administrators** group and press the **Update** button:

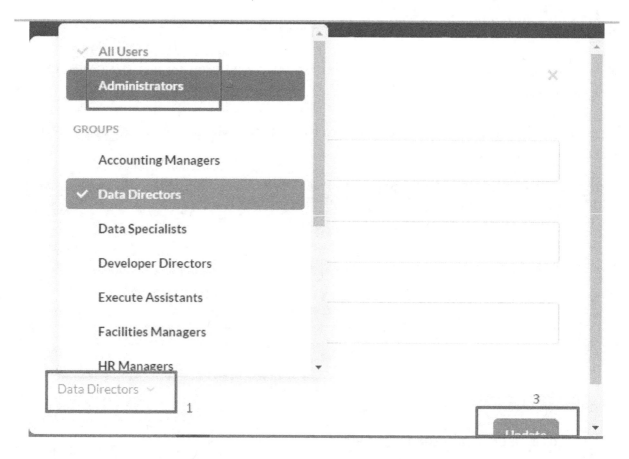

Figure 105. Assigning a user to be an administrator

Then on the **People** setting page, we will see the user account has been updated

Figure 106. A user has been added to Administrators

Setting the Data Specialist permissions

The next thing is to set up permissions for Data Specialists. We stated in our rule that Data Specialists can access and write raw SQL on all databases.

Navigate to **Admin > Permissions > Data permissions**, scroll to the **Data Specialist** column:

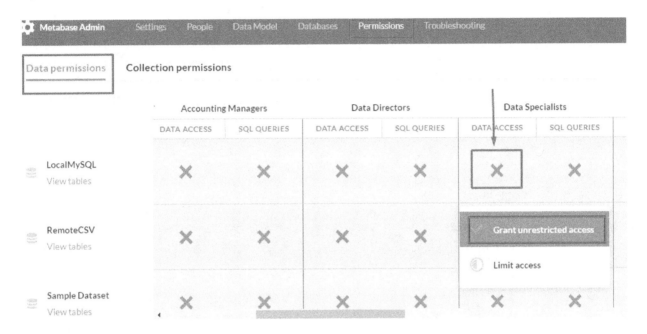

Figure 107. Grant unrestricted access to Data Specialists

Click the **X** button in the **Data Access** column and select **Grant unrestricted access**. Now click the **SQL Queries** column and select **Write raw queries**

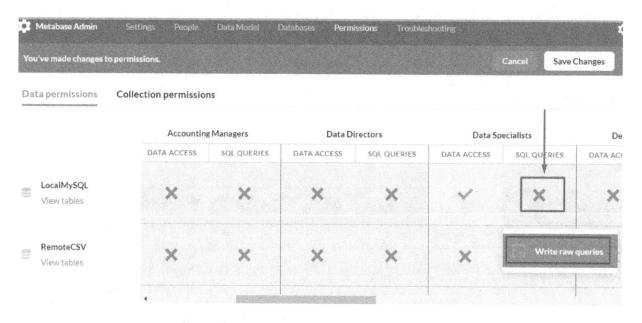

Figure 108. Assigning write raw queries permission

Then save the changes:

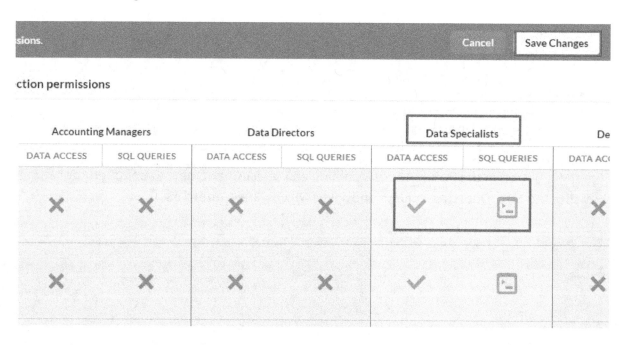

Figure 109. Saving the changes

Finally, confirm the changes:

Save permissions?

Data Specialists will be given access to 4 tables in Sample Dataset.
Data Specialists will now be able to write native queries for Sample Dataset.
Data Specialists will be given access to 3 tables in RemoteCSV.
Data Specialists will now be able to write native queries for RemoteCSV.
Data Specialists will be given access to 1 table in LocalMySQL.
Data Specialists will now be able to write native queries for LocalMySQL.

Are you sure you want to do this?

Cancel

Figure 110. Confirming the changes

Setting other groups permissions

For other groups such as President, Execute Assistant, and VP we will need to assign permissions to them in the collection setting page.

I will describe in more detail when we finish organizing our collections for the company. Now we just skip this part.

4.6. Where is the delete button?

So you want to delete objects like user accounts, reports, groups… but you can't find the delete button?

Metabase has no concept of deletion. So you shouldn't waste your time finding a way to delete an object.

Instead of that, it has some functionalities like deactivation/reactivation and archiving. For example, you can only deactivate a user and reactivate this inactive user.

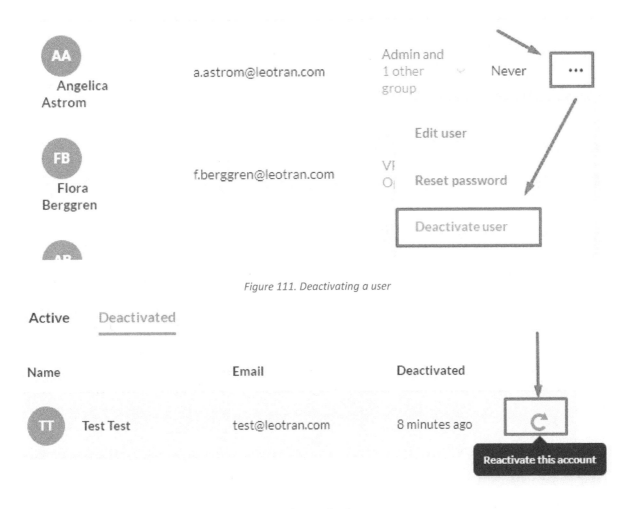

Figure 111. Deactivating a user

Figure 112. Reactivating a user

There is no way to completely delete a user on the web interface in **Metabase** even if you're logging in as an administrator.

Some of my readers may think about modifying **Metabase's** backend database to delete users.

I don't recommend you tweak **Metabase's** database as it could damage your **Metabase**. Things went critical if the **Metabase** is the main reporting system in your company.

If you still want to tweak the database, I suggest several things you need to do before starting your modification:

- Have at least one latest backup of the database.
- Understand clearly the **Metabase's** database structure.
- Test the changes in the test and staging before applying to the production environment.

You can only be able to archive a collection

Figure 113. Archiving a collection

4.7. References

- https://www.metabase.com/docs/latest/
-

Chapter 5: Analytics, Collections, and Reports

In previous chapter you have done create users and permission scheme for the whole reporting system based on the rule of permissions, and the corporate's structure. In this chapter, I will show you how to organize the reporting system in a clean and extensible way.

5.1. The overall structure

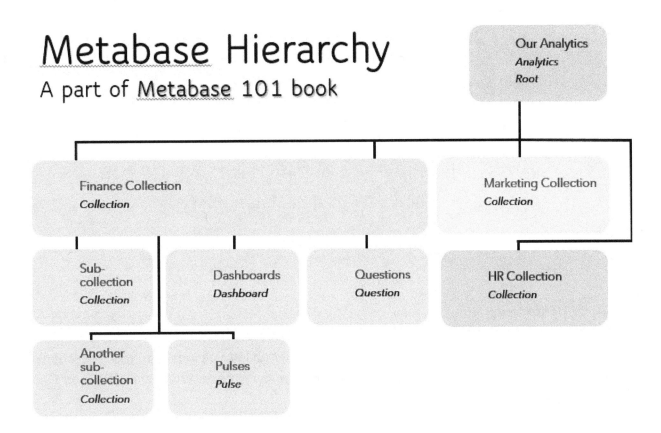

Figure 114. The Metabase hierarchy

Since **Metabase** uses its own concepts, these concepts may confuse readers/users for the first time so I have made a conversion table as below

Metabase concept	Equivalent word
Analytics	Root dir
Collections	Directories
Dashboard	Report page
Questions	Queries
Pulses	Triggers/Jobs

Figure 115. The Metabase concept conversion table

5.2. Analytics

Metabase has one and only one container named **Our Analytics** where all your collections are located. Analytics has the same role as workspace or root directory/container. You can't create/delete/modify the analytics.

You can create as many collections as you need inside **Analytics**.

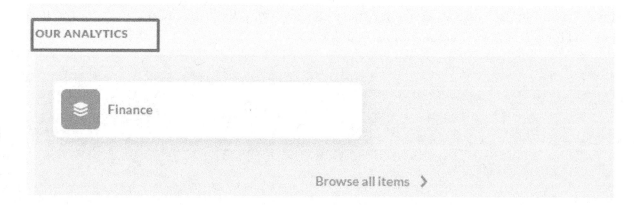

Figure 116. Our Analytics

Please remember that **Analytics** can contain only **Collections**.

5.3. Collections

Collections are the smaller level of container compared to **Analytics** where sub-collections, dashboard, questions, and pulses are located.

By default, there will be:

- 2 collections named **My personal collections** and **All personal collections** for administrators
- 1 collection named **My personal collections** for other normal users

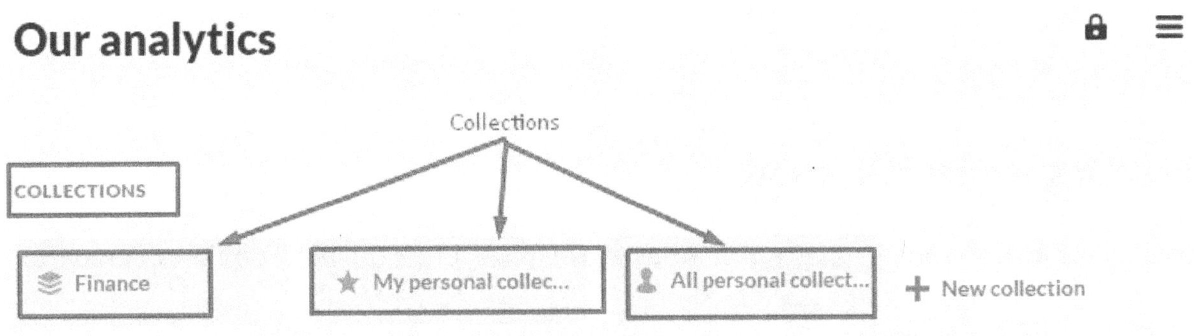

Figure 117. Collections

You can't change the name of these default collections even if you are logging in as an administrator.

Think **Analytics** and **Collections** are just folders/directories in a directory hierarchy. **Analytics** is the root directory. **Collections** are sub-directories.

You can create as many levels of sub-collection as you need inside a collection

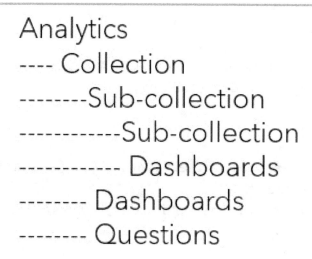

Figure 118. Sub-collections inside a collection

Creating a new collection

To create a new collection, on the **Our Analytics** page, press the **New collection** button

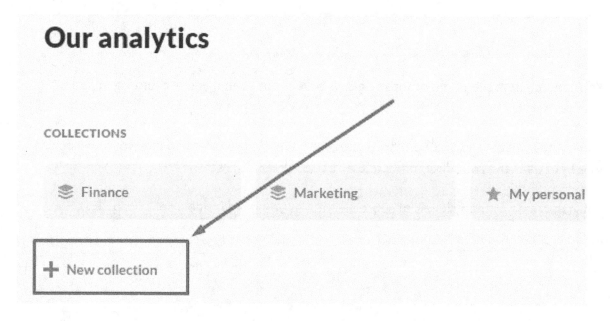

Figure 119. Creating a new collection

A dialog appears, fill the collection information into the form

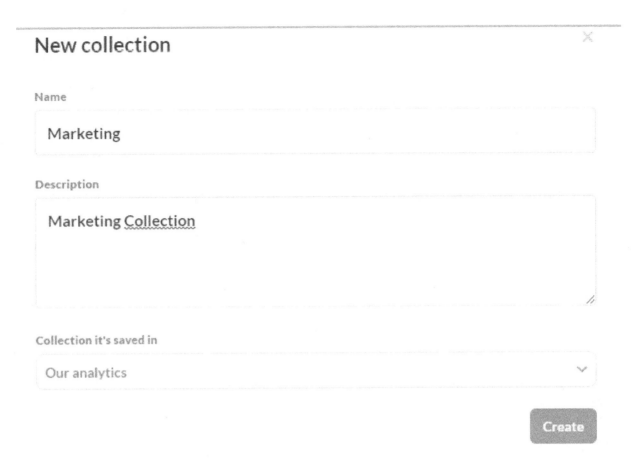

Figure 120. A new collection dialog

5.4. Dashboards

Dashboards are the report pages. **Dashboards** are the result of your work what your boss will look at every time he needs to see the report.

Dashboards must be located inside a collection. Multiple collections can share a dashboard.

Dashboards usually are in the **Dashboards** tab inside a collection.

All objects including dashboards, questions, pulses will be visible in the **Everything** tab.

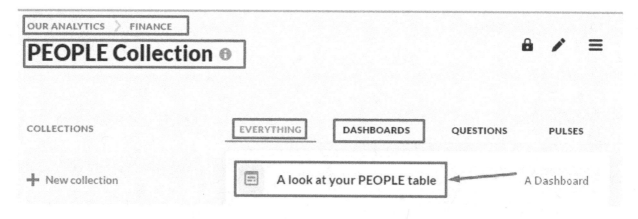

Figure 121. A Dashboard inside a collection

If you choose to pin a dashboard, it will be at the top of the collection instead of at the **Dashboard** tab.

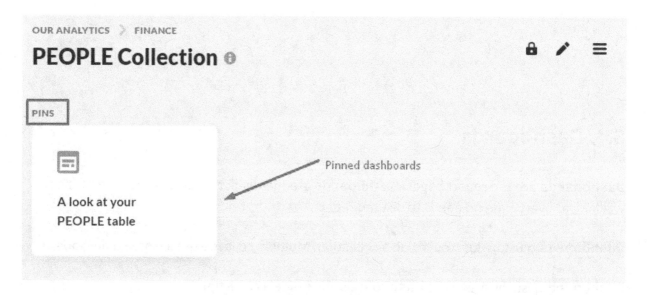

Figure 122. Pinned dashboards

To create a new dashboard, click the plus button on the navigation bar

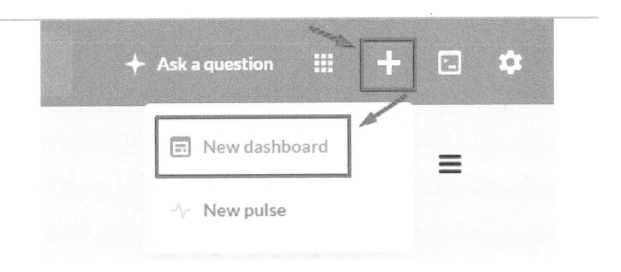

Figure 123. Creating a new dashboard

Creating a new dashboard

Press the **New dashboard** button as the above guide, you will have a dialog appears, fill in the form:

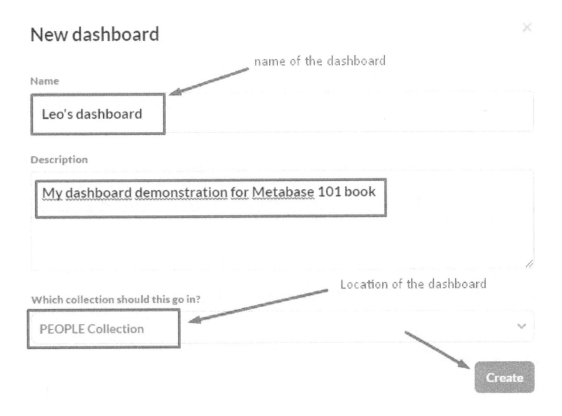

Figure 124. A new dashboard dialog

You will have a new empty dashboard. Click the edit button (the pen icon) to edit the dashboard

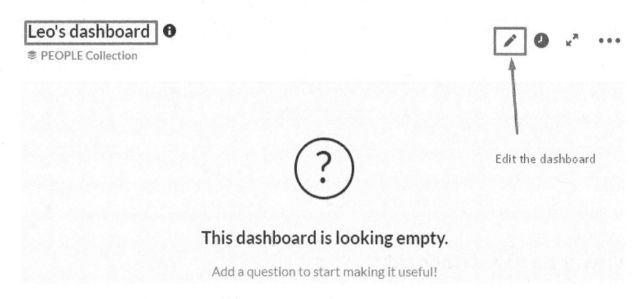

Figure 125. A new empty dashboard created

Now press the plus button to add a new question to the dashboard

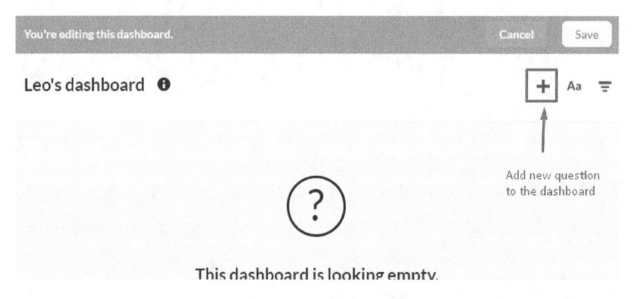

Figure 126. Adding a new question to the dashboard

A Pickup dialog appears, now select the question you need

Figure 127. Picking a question to add to a dashboard

Now you will have the question result on the dashboard

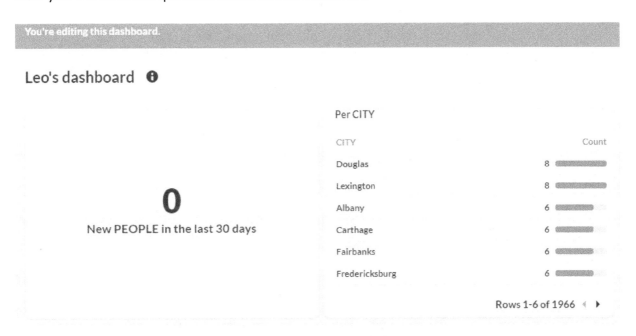

Figure 128. Questions on the dashboard

Finally, press the **Save** button to save the changes made to the dashboard.

5.5. Questions

`Questions` are the specific queries to get the specific result. A **dashboard** usually contains multiple questions to provide a unique view of the report's subject.

E.g. a report/dashboard about people in the company required by the HR department may have some questions about:

- New people in the last 30 days?
- New people per month?
- All people grouped by coordinates, by cities?
- Total number of people in the company?

All these questions can be gathered inside a dashboard to form a report about the human resources of the company.

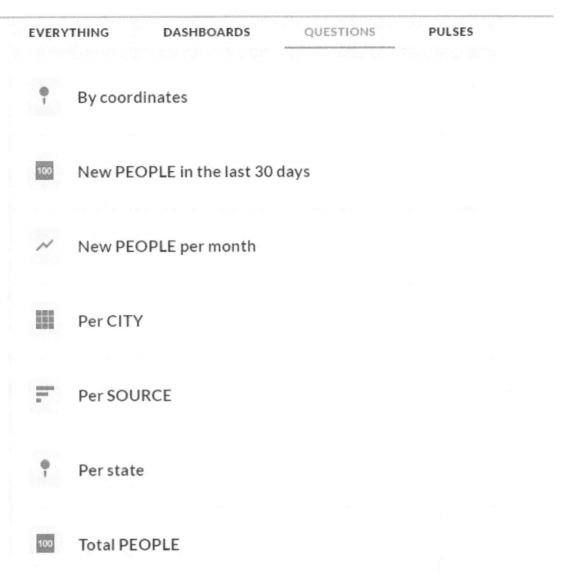

Figure 129. Questions inside a collection

The dashboard then will have a look like this

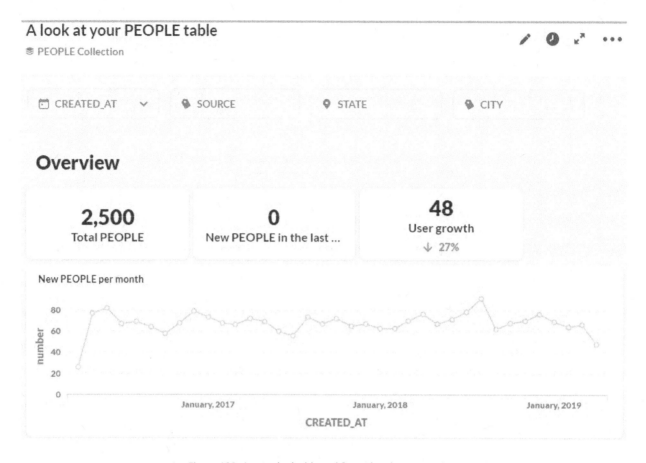

Figure 130. A sample dashboard from the above questions

It is a very intuitive interface that your separated numbers finally be displayed in a meaningful way thanks to **Metabase**.

To create a new question, press the **Ask a question** button on the navigation bar

Figure 131. Asking a new question

Creating a new question

Press the **Ask a question** button as the above guide, depend on the permissions of your account, you will be redirected to a new question page as below:

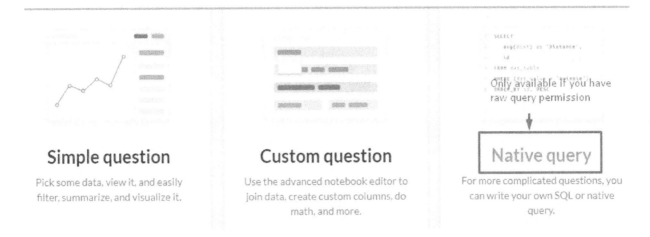

Simple question

Pick some data, view it, and easily filter, summarize, and visualize it.

Custom question

Use the advanced notebook editor to join data, create custom columns, do math, and more.

Native query

For more complicated questions, you can write your own SQL or native query.

Figure 132. Creating a new question

I myself usually use the native raw query for the report but I will introduce the native query later. In this section, I will guide you with the **Simple** question option. Click the **Simple question** button and pick the **Sample Dataset** as your data.

Figure 133. Picking a database

Select the **PEOPLE** table and wait a little for the data to be fetched then click the **Summarize** button

Figure 134. Summarize a table

Now select **Count** and press the **Done** button:

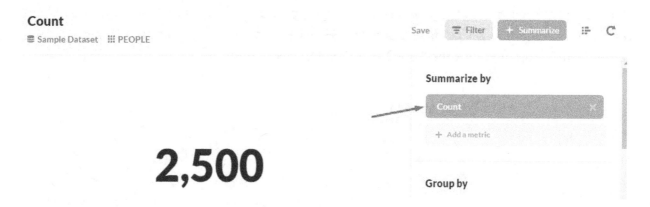

Figure 135. Selecting count summarize

You will have your result of the query on the left. Now press the **Save** button and fill in the question information:

Figure 136. Saving the question

A dialog will appear to ask you to add this question to a dashboard. Click **Not now**. Take a look at the **PEOPLE** collection we will see our newly created question with the description

Figure 137. The new question with a description

5.6. Pulses

Pulses are scheduled jobs on the questions. You can use pulses to set up a scheduled job to send the report to your team by email or Slack notification.

To create a new pulse, click the plus button on the navigation bar

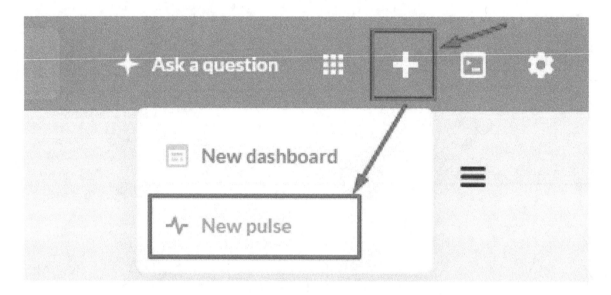

Figure 138. Creating a new pulse

Creating a new pulse

To create a new pulse you'll need:

- The destination: Configured email (section 3.2) or/and Slack (section 3.3) before so **Metabase** have some ways to send the data to. Please take a look at chapter 3 for more information about basic configurations for **Metabase**.
- The data: At least one question exists to provide the data to the pulse.

Now press the **New pulse** button then you will be redirected to the new pulse page.

New pulse

What's a Pulse?

Name your pulse

Give your pulse a name to help others understand what it's about.

People report   ← Name of the pulse

Which collection should this pulse live in?

Location of
the pulse

PEOPLE Collection   ←   ⌄

Figure 139. Creating a new pulse

Pick your data

Choose questions you'd like to send in this pulse.

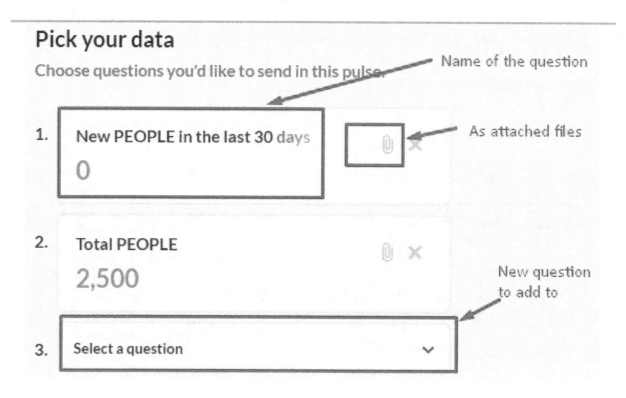

Figure 140. Creating a new pulse (2)

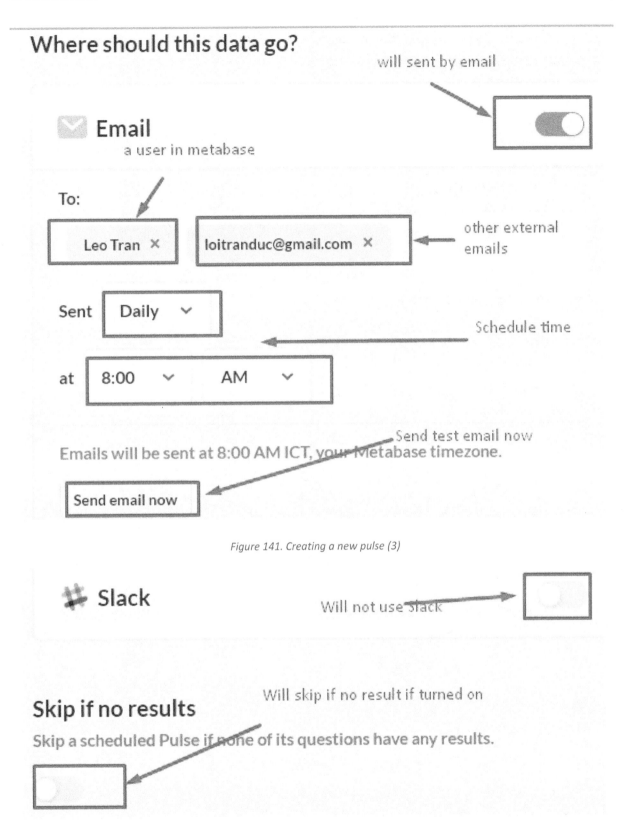

Figure 141. Creating a new pulse (3)

Figure 142. Creating a new pulse (4)

Press the **Create Pulse** button then navigate to the **People** collection, press the **PULSES** tab to see the pulse has been created successfully

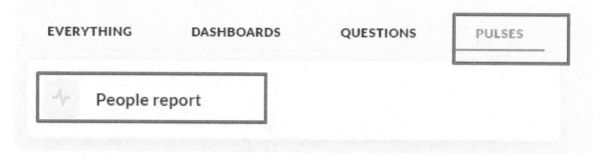

Figure 143. Checking the created pulse inside a collection

Your pulse email will look something like this:

People report

New PEOPLE in the last 30 days
0

Total PEOPLE
2,500

Figure 144. A Pulse sent by email

5.7. Organizing the corporate's report system

Now you can understand the most basic parts of **Metabase**, we need to organize things so we can scale up and be ready for the complex reporting system of a company.

I will set up **Metabase** analytics based on the company structure (section 4.1). Please take a look back at the organization chart if you don't remember. The result will be something like this:

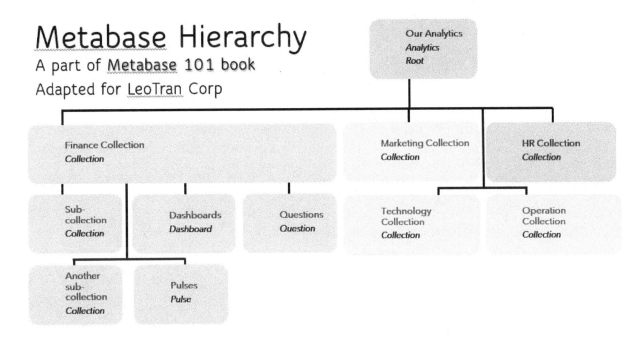

Figure 145. The Metabase hierarchy for LeoTran Corp

Our analytics will be something like this:

Figure 146. Our analytics layout

5.8. Setting up permissions for a collection

In the previous chapter, I wrote that we will set up permissions based on <u>our rule of permissions</u> for each collection. Now we will set up the permission for Finance collection. Go to **Finance collection**, press the lock button:

Figure 147. The set permission button

The permissions for the Finance collection dialog appears, based on the rule of permissions, we'll set the permissions as below table:

Group name	Permission
Data Director	Curate collection
Data Specialist	Curate collection
VP Finance	View collection
Accounting Manager	View collection
Execute Assistant	View collection
President	View collection

Figure 148. Group names and permissions

Set the permissions:

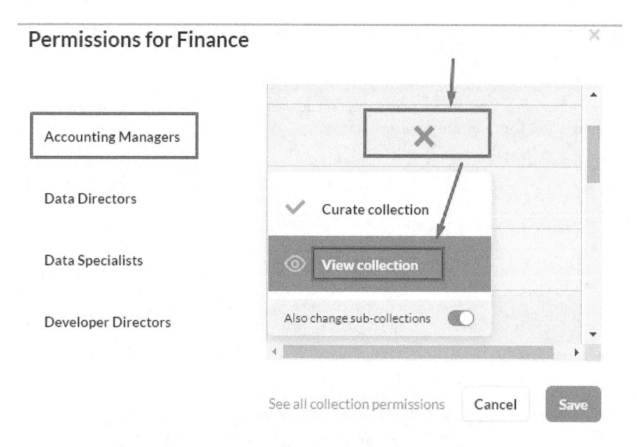

Figure 149. Setting permissions for each group

Do the same for other groups then press the **Save** button to finish editing.

Repeat above tasks to other collections we will have our analytics layout created and set permissions up completely compliant with <u>our rule of permissions</u>.

5.9. References

- https://www.metabase.com/docs/latest/
-

Chapter 6: Advanced Metabase

In previous chapter you have learned the basic elements of **Metabase** and also create some simple questions then add to the dashboard. In this chapter, we will focus on some advanced topics including XRAY, native query, region map, pin map, data hiding, troubleshooting, and multi-instance synchronization.

6.1. Creating a dashboard with XRAY

XRAY is the lighting fast way to create a dashboard within just few clicks. **Metabase** will automatically create questions and a dashboard based on the data of the table.

To create a dashboard with **XRAY**, first choose a data source from the **Our Data** page

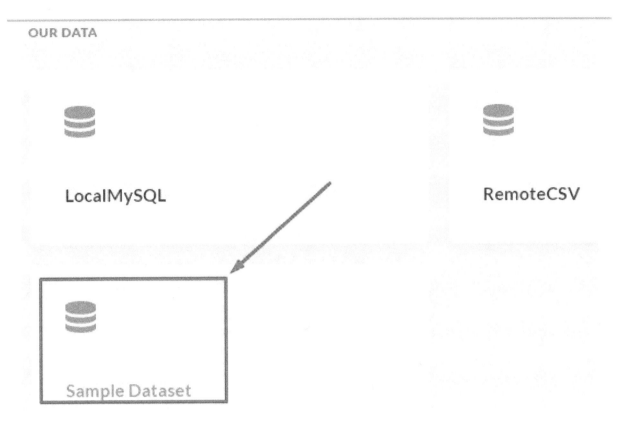

Figure 150. Choosing a data source

Choose the flash button beside the table

Figure 151. The XRAY of a table

Wait for a while for **Metabase** to generate an **XRAY** dashboard

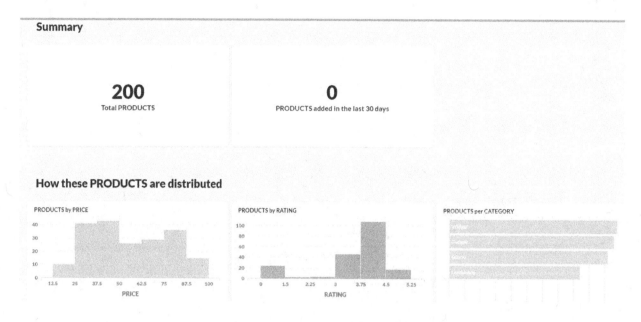

Figure 152. An example XRAY dashboard

You will have something like this, press the **Save** button to save the dashboard.

6.2. Creating a question with Native Query

By far, we have done creating a question with the Simple question in Chapter 5. This method is useful only in some simple cases. To have full control and creating more complex reports, I suggest you use **Native Query**.

Create a new question and choose the **Native Query** button

Figure 153. The Native query button

Select the desired dataset:

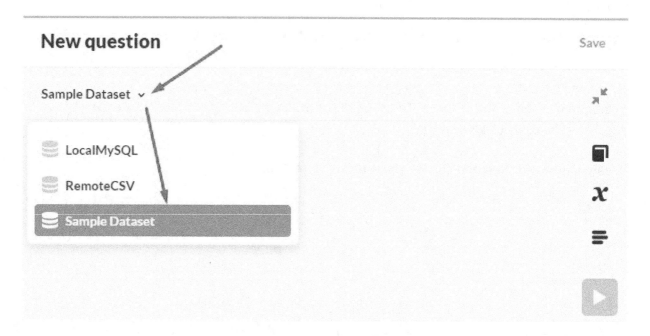

Figure 154. Selecting the database for the query

In this case, I will choose the **Sample Dataset**. To see the dataset structure (e.g. tables, columns) press the **Learn about your data** button on the right side

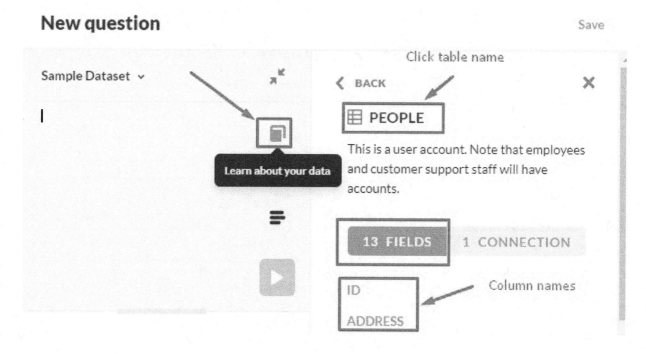

Figure 155. Learning about the data

Now write the query and press the **Run** button

Figure 156. Writing a SQL and running inside Metabase

You will have something like this:

Figure 157. A query's result

Now we will modify the visualization of the result by clicking the **Visualization** button

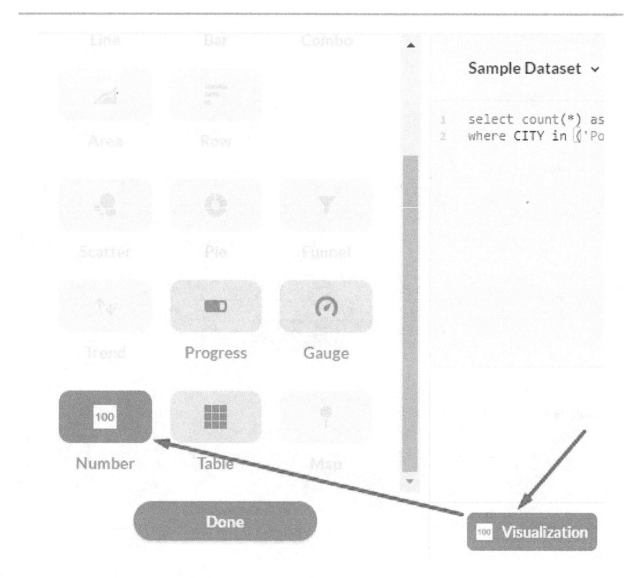

Figure 158. Changing the visualization

We can see that based on the result of the query, **Metabase** automatically chooses the display type for us. In this case, it's a **Number** type.

We also notice that there are four available display types for this kind of data including **Number**, **Table**, **Progress,** and **Gauge**. The other display formats might not suit the result hence Metabase has blurred them.

Choose **Progress** and configure as below to see the changes

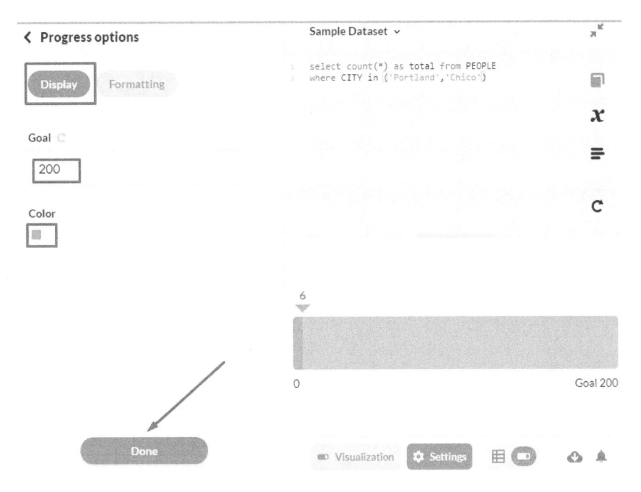

Figure 159. The progress options

Press the **Done** button if you choose this layout. Try again with the **Gauge** option:

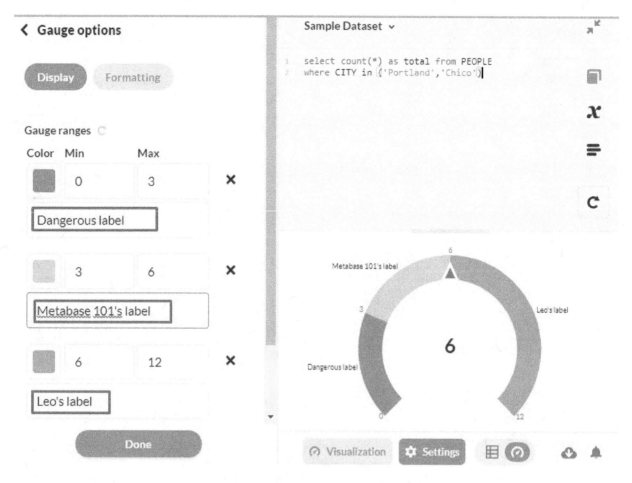

Figure 160. The Gauge options

Finally, click the **Save** button to save the question. A familiar dialog is displayed, fill the question information into the form. We will save the question in the HR collection.

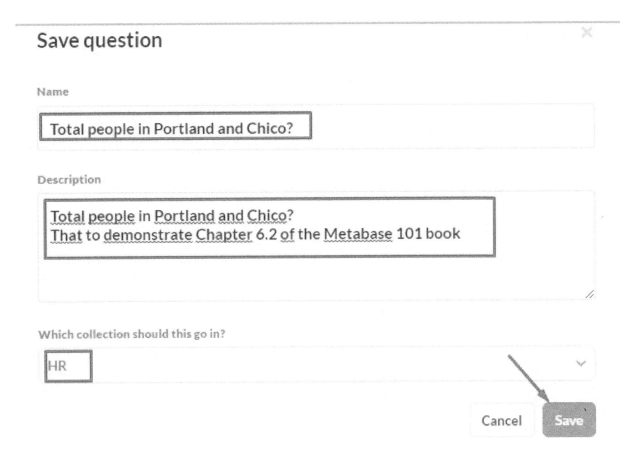

Figure 161. Saving the question

Choose **Not now** to skip adding to a dashboard.

6.3. Creating a question with Region Map

First question, what is a region map?

To answer this, open the **Metabase** then create an XRAY dashboard (see section 6.1) on the
Sample Dataset > **PEOPLE** table you will have a dashboard like this:

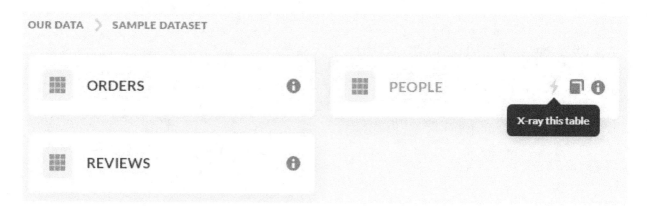

Figure 162. Creating an XRAY dashboard

Scroll down until you see this part:

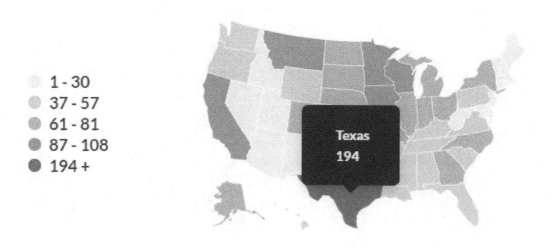

Figure 163. An example of a region map

This is a Region Map.

Region Map is one of the most efficient ways to display your data to viewers when your data is related to location.

By default, **Metabase** has mapped all states in the United States, so if you make reports with locations in the United States, you don't have to add the map manually.

If you have a report with locations located all around the world, you have to add the map manually. In order to add the map manually you need 4 conditions:

- Have the **geojson** file in a proper format of the region.
- A Github or any file server that stores the **geojson** file.
- Make sure the **Metabase** server can access the **geojson** file URL.
- Make sure the clients (the machines which openning the **Metabase** web interface) can access the **geojson** file URL.

Finding the desired region geojson file

It's not easy to find a **geojson** file on the internet nowadays. In this example, I will guide you to download a **geojson** file from the internet. In the next section, I will guide you to create the **geojson** map your own with any region you want.

The sample geojson file can be grabbed here:

https://raw.githubusercontent.com/Vizzuality/growasia_calculator/master/public/vietnam.geo json

This **geojson** is a part of the **Grow Asia Carbon Emissions Calculator**'s Github at: https://github.com/Vizzuality/growasia_calculator

Please note that you don't have to download the **geojson** file to your local machine in case you are planning to use Github as your **geojson** file server. In this book, we'll use the github as the file server to store the **geojson** file.

Adding the custom map

Go to **Admin** > **Settings** > **Maps** click the **Add a map** button

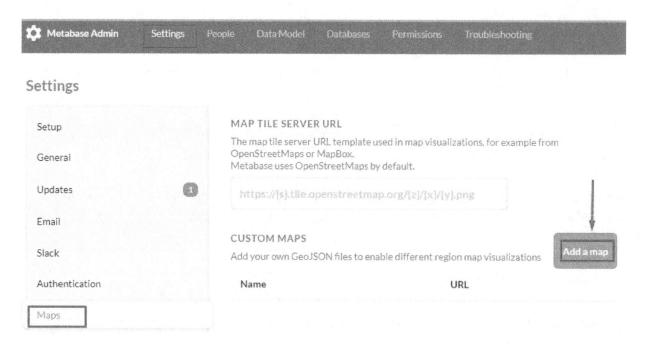

Figure 164. Adding a custom map

Fill the information in the displayed form

Figure 165. Filling in the map's information

Press the **Load** button to load the map. Wait for the map to be loaded then choose the identifier and the display name

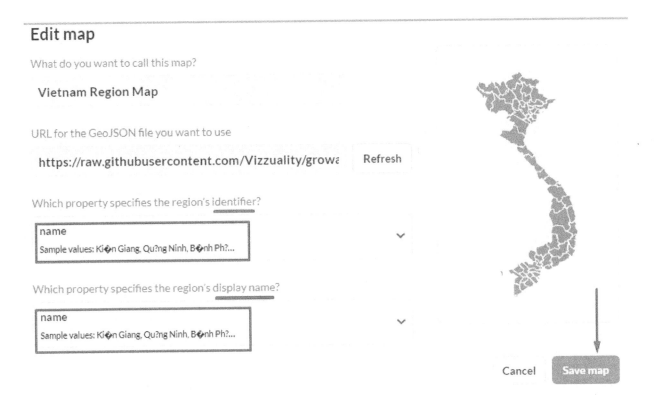

Figure 166. Configuring the map identifier and display name

(i) Depends on your map size and your internet connection, you may need to wait for a while for the data to be fully loaded.

Press the **Add map** button to save the map. Now create a table with some data like this

DBEU · METABASE · CITIES

CITY	LAT	LNG	POP
Hồ Chí Minh city	10.81670000° N	106.63330000° E	13,312,000
Hà Nội	21.02450000° N	105.84120000° E	7,785,000
Alabama			4,903,185
Alaska			731,545
Arizona			7,278,717
California			39,512,223
Hải Phòng			2,103,500
Cần Thơ			1,237,300
Đồng Nai			1,104,000
Nam Định			352,108

Figure 167. A simple cities table

Now create a native query question (section 6.2) with the query "`select * from METABASE.CITIES`" then in the **Visualization** choose Map layout

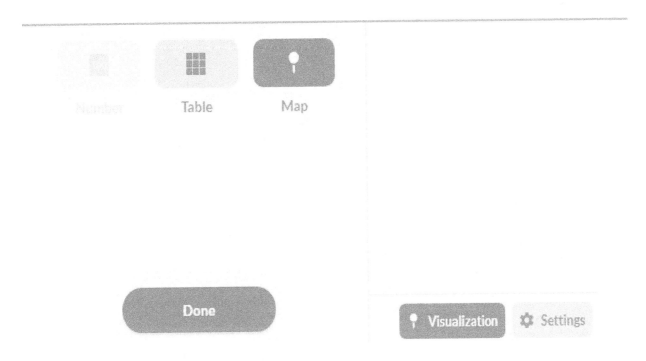

Figure 168. Choosing the Map layout

Now in the **Map Options** choose the **Vietnam Region Map** that has been created earlier

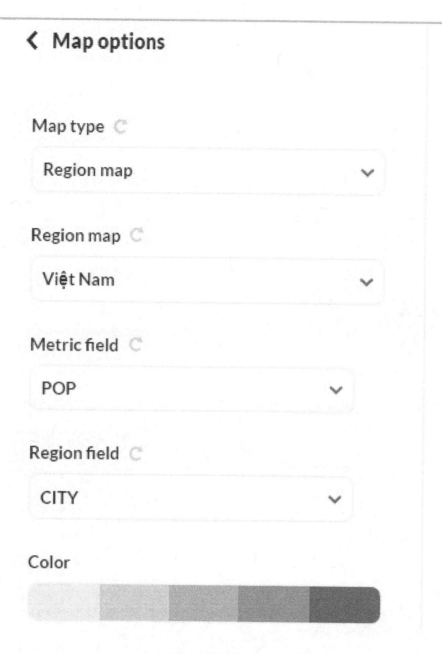

Figure 169. Filling the map options

We will have something like this:

CITIES

352.1k - 2.1M
4.9M
7.3M - 7.8M
13.3M
39.5M +

Figure 170. A sample region map

Because we chose the Vietnam map, the United States regions such as Alabama, Alaska… can't be displayed.

Switch to the United States map, you can see that Ha Noi and Ho Chi Minh City shall not be displayed.

6.4. Creating a custom region map

We need to find somehow to create custom maps and I will show you in this section. First of all, navigate to OpenStreetMap: https://umap.openstreetmap.fr/en/ and press the **Create a map** button:

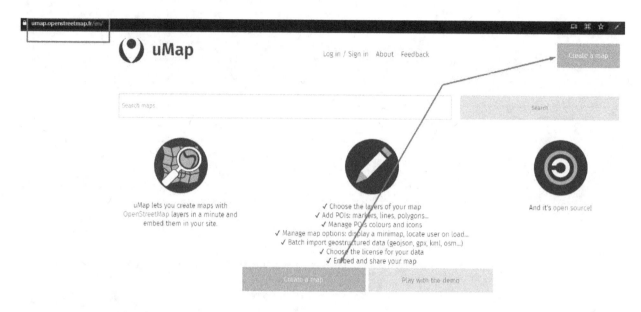

Figure 171. The UMap website

Umap is an **OpenStreetMap's** project that lets you create your own map easily right on the web interface.

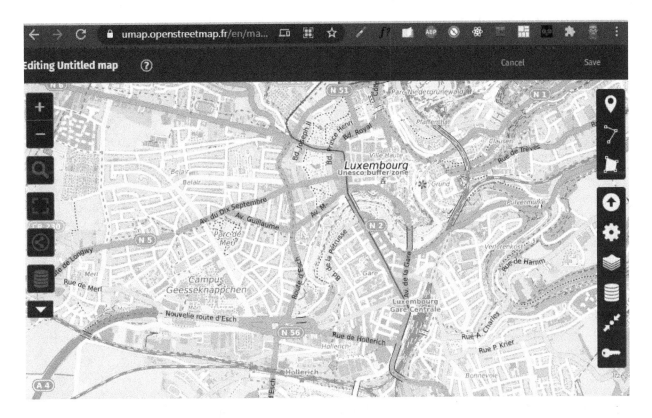

Figure 172. Creating a new map in UMap

You can see an unnamed map with a toolbox on the right side. Here I will choose a small region of **Luxembourg** near **Luxembourg Gare Centrale**, it is for demonstration and you can change the region yourself. Now select the polygon tool on the right side and start to draw a polygonal region on the map.

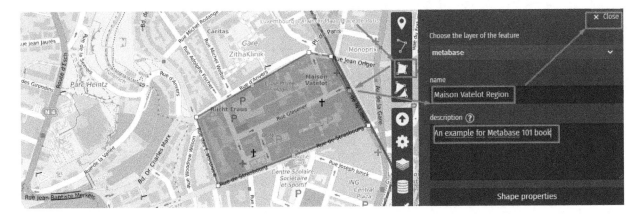

Figure 173. Drawing a polygon

When you have completed drawing the polygon there will be a dialog slides from the right side allow you to enter the polygon properties. When you finish filling in the form, press the **Close** button to save the changes.

Please note that I have chosen the polygon that will be saved on the layer named **metabase** that I have created before. To create a new layer press the **Add a layer** button:

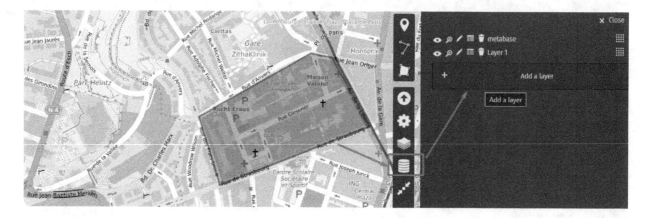

Figure 174. Adding a new layer

You don't have to create a new layer to save the polygon, it will be added automatically to the **Layer 1**. Now export the polygon data:

Figure 175. Exporting the map

Choose the format of the exporting data to be **geojson** then download the file to the local machine. The next step is to push the geojson file onto a file server so that **Metabase** can access this map. I have done this step already and uploaded the file to Github with the

following URL:
https://raw.githubusercontent.com/loitd/metabase101/main/chapter06/Maison-Vatelot.geojson.

You can also preview the region in Github.com:

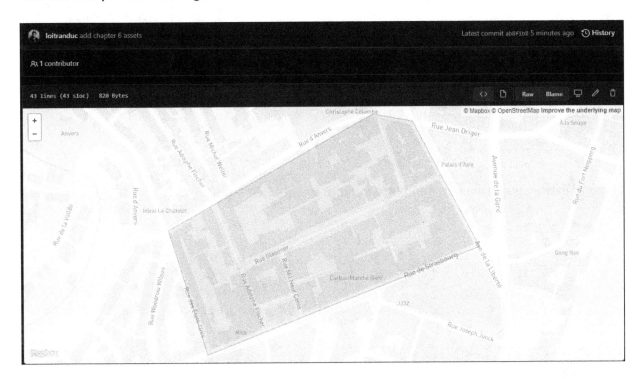

Figure 176. Previewing the region map on github.com

Yes, it's exactly the polygon that we draw earlier.

Go back to the **Metabase**, add a custom map named `Maison Vatelot Region`

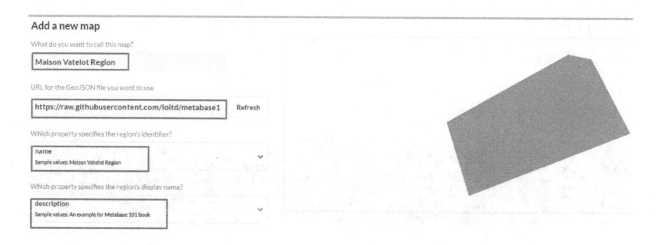

Figure 177. Adding the custom map

Congratulation, you have done adding a custom map to **Metabase**.

6.5. Creating a Pin Map

What is a Pin map?

To answer this, reopen the XRAY dashboard we've created in section 6.3, scroll down and find this part

Figure 178. An example of a PIN map

This is a Pin map.

To form a pin map our data tables need longitude and latitude information. Take a look at an example table below:

Figure 179. Example data of a table source of a PIN map

The longitude and latitude columns can be the text type but they should be formatted as **Float** (MySQL) or **Real** (SQLite). You have to set the **Data modeling** of these fields to longitude and latitude

Figure 180. Modeling the data

Now refresh the **Metabase** dataset browse page to have longitude and latitude signs added:

Figure 181. Refreshing the dataset on the Metabase web interface

How to get the geolocation

You can get the geolocation using **uMap**, go back to <u>the custom region map created on uMap in section 6.4</u> and use the marker tool to create a pin on the map

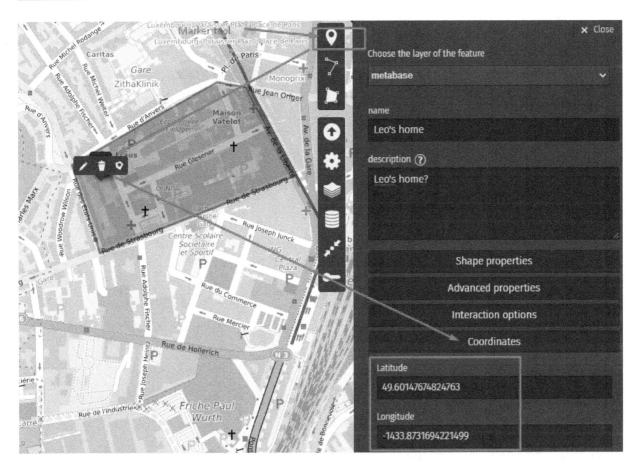

Figure 182. Get the geolocation on UMap

Select marker tool and place it on the map, a dialog slides from the right side, press the **Coordinates** button to see the geolocation.

In the above image, the longitude and latitude are:

Latitude: 49.60147674824763

Long: -1433.8731694221499

Another way to get the long/lat data is to get them directly from **OpenStreetMap.org**

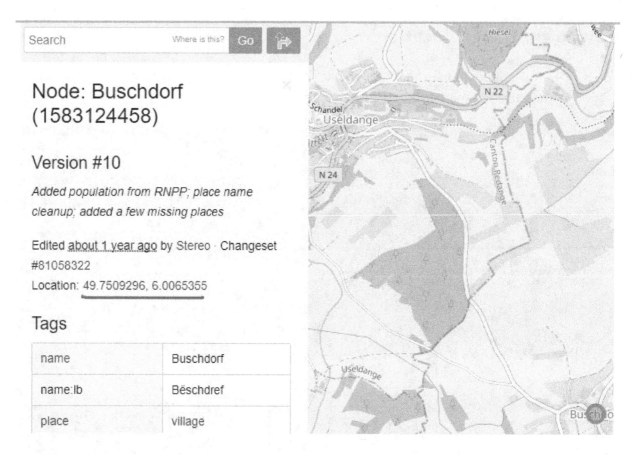

Figure 183. Getting the geolocation on OpenStreetMap

How to create a Pin map

As I said earlier we need to have a table with the data looks like this:

Metabase SQLite • Emp

ID	Email	Longitude	Latitude
1	leo@leo.com	6.08488083° E	49.79112808° N
3	test@test.com	6.00574493° E	49.75132720° N

Figure 184. A Pin map sample data

Now choose **Ask a question > Simple > Database Name > Schema Name > Table EMP** (the table with the data above)

Choose the **Visualization** with the below settings:

Figure 185. Configuring the Pin map options

Press the **Save** button to save the question with Pin map data.

6.6. Data Model and Data hiding

In section 6.5 I have written about how to use a data model to format the longitude and latitude of a table, in this section we will use data modeling to hide data globally. With a data model, you have 2 options to hide data:

- Hide the whole table
- Hide one or some column in the table

First, go to **Admin > Data Model** and select the dataset

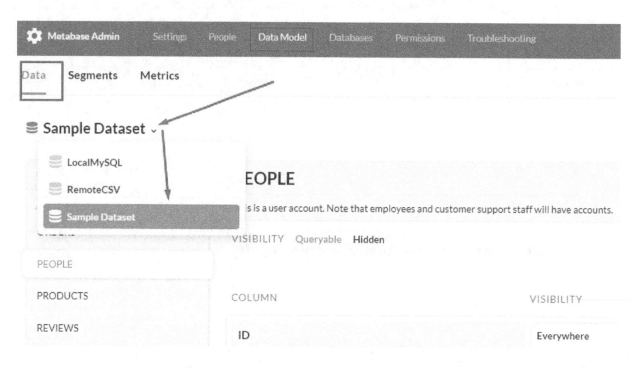

Figure 186. Data modeling of a table

Now choose a table and press the **Hidden** button to hide the whole table:

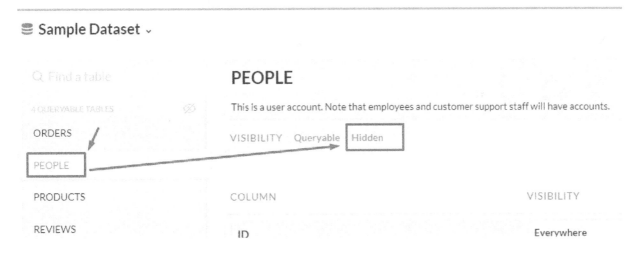

Figure 187. Hiding a table

To switch it back to the visible state, press the **Queryable** button.

To hide a column from queries select the **Do not include** in the drop-down of the **visibility** select.

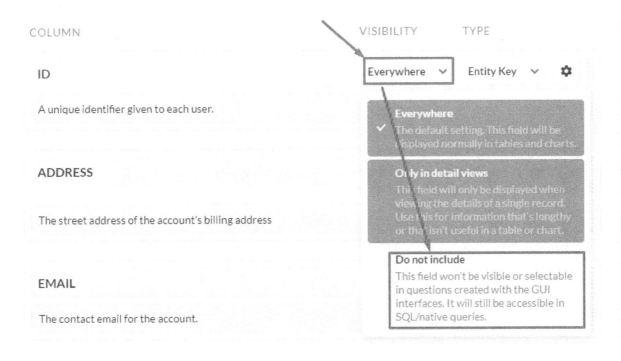

Figure 188. Hiding a column

This field will be invisible in all reports but still be able to access in the Native queries. By default, all columns and tables in **Metabase** are visible and accessible from anywhere.

To hide columns right in the questions, without accessing the Data model, go to a table view of the question and press the **Settings** button:

Figure 189. Hiding a column in a report

A dialog will slide from the left side, press the **X** button to hide the desired column. Press the **Done** button to save your modification.

This kind of setting helps you hide the columns just in a specific report while the setting in the Data model helps you to hide the columns from the whole system.

6.7. Metabase troubleshooting

It is essential for any system to have a log for administrators to debug the application. In chapter 1, I have introduced how to view the log right in the console while running with a JAR file, the log in the console will be something like this:

```
2021-03-03 16:43:15,525 INFO metabase.task :: Initializing task SyncDatabases
2021-03-03 16:43:15,880 INFO metabase.task :: Initializing task CheckForNewVersions
2021-03-03 16:43:15,955 INFO metabase.task :: Initializing task SendAnonymousUsageStats
2021-03-03 16:43:16,076 INFO metabase.task :: Initializing task SendAbandomentEmails
2021-03-03 16:43:16,115 INFO metabase.task :: Initializing task SendPulses
2021-03-03 16:43:16,245 INFO metabase.task :: Initializing task SendFollowUpEmails
2021-03-03 16:43:16,510 INFO metabase.task :: Initializing task TaskHistoryCleanup
2021-03-03 16:43:16,614 INFO metabase.core :: Metabase Initialization COMPLETE
2021-03-03 16:43:21,825 INFO i18n.impl :: Reading available locales from locales.clj...
```

Figure 190. The Metabase console log

But **Metabase** has another place to view the log so you don't have to worry even in the case that you can't access the console view.

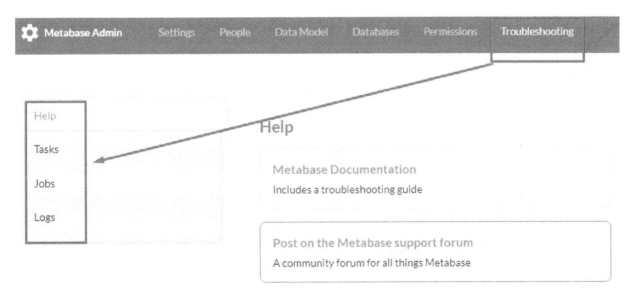

Figure 191. The Metabase troubleshooting page

Go to **Admin > Troubleshooting**, you will see the right menu with some items.

General information

To view the information about the current running Metabase instance, in the **Help** page, scroll down to the **Diagnostic Info** section.

Diagnostic Info

Please include these details in support requests. Thank you!

```
{
    "browser-info": {
        "language": "en-US",
        "platform": "Win32",
        "userAgent": "Mozilla/5.0 (Windows NT 10.0; Win64; x64) AppleWebKit/537.36 (KHTML, like Gecko)
Chrome/90.0.4430.212 Safari/537.36",
        "vendor": "Google Inc."
    },
    "system-info": {
        "file.encoding": "Cp1252",
        "java.runtime.name": "Java(TM) SE Runtime Environment",
        "java.runtime.version": "1.8.0_281-b09",
        "java.vendor": "Oracle Corporation",
```

Figure 192. The Metabase general information

All the information of the instance will be shown so you can have an overview of your instance.

Tasks & Jobs

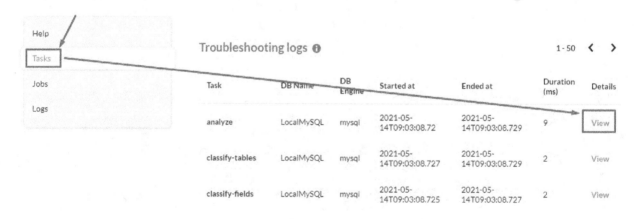

Figure 193. Metabase tasks

Periodically, **Metabase** will do tasks including your scheduled pulses and the system's jobs. The **Tasks** menu shows both periodical and non-periodical tasks.

			2021-05-	2021-05-		
send-pulses			14T09:00:00.005	14T09:00:00.04	35	View
				Pulses		
task-history-cleanup			2021-05-14T09:00:00.011	2021-05-14T09:00:00.04	29	View
classify-tables	Sample Dataset	h2	2021-05-14T08:50:00.27	2021-05-14T08:50:00.275	5	View
			System jobs			
analyze	Sample Dataset	h2	2021-05-14T08:50:00.252	2021-05-14T08:50:00.275	23	View
classify-fields	Sample Dataset	h2	2021-05-14T08:50:00.265	2021-05-14T08:50:00.27	5	View

Figure 194. A Metabase tasks page

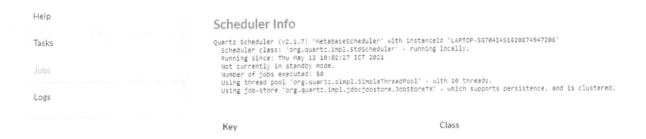

Figure 195. A Metabase jobs page

We can see that this instance uses Quartz Scheduler v2.1.7.

Logs

Last but not least is the **Logs** page which has all the logs of **Metabase**

Figure 196. The Metabase logs page

6.8. Multi-instance synchronization

When running in K8s or any environment with multiple instances for load balancing, you may face lagging between **Metabase** instances while performing heavy tasks such as: Adding a new big custom map, rescanning a big table...

```
DEBUG metabase.middleware.log PUT /api/setting/query-caching-ttl-ratio 204 10.6 ms (4 DB calls) App DB connect
DEBUG metabase.middleware.log GET /api/setting 200 1.5 ms (0 DB calls) App DB connections: 0/13 Jetty threads:
DEBUG metabase.middleware.log GET /api/session/properties 200 4.3 ms (2 DB calls) App DB connections: 0/13 Jet
DEBUG metabase.middleware.log GET /api/util/bug_report_details 200 5.0 ms (1 DB calls) App DB connections: 0/1
INFO metabase.models.setting.cache Settings have been changed on another instance, and will be reloaded here.
```

Figure 197. A Metabase multi-instance log

You can check the **Troubleshooting > Logs** to see the lagging message as above picture. In this case, all you need to do is to wait for a while until all instances have been synchronized successfully.

Appendix 1: List of figures

Appendix 2: List of examples

No table of figures entries found.